DEER CREEK

Deer Creek

THE MURDERS OF WILLIAM H. GIBSON AND JOHN S. FRAZER

D.A. Chadwick

WordMerchant Publications

Contents

dedication	viii
Acknowledgements	1
Characters Involved in the Frazer and Gibson Murder Investigations	2

Prologue   31

One
History of Howard, Elk and Chautauqua Counties   37

Two
Kansas, the Cattle Industry and Tick Fever   42

Three
The Murder of William Harrison Gibson   49

Four
The Murder and Inquest of John Samuel Frazer   73

Five
The Investigation Begins in Chautauqua County 1890   79

Six
The Elk and Chautauqua County Investigations 1890-1893   91

Seven
More Arrests in 1894   100

Eight
March 16, 1896 at Sedan, Chautauqua County   115

Nine
The Testimony of John F. New   122

Ten
Further Testimony on March 18, 1896 Chautauqua
County, Kansas   131

Eleven
The Trials Begin 1895 and 1896   139

Twelve
The Role of the Media and Politics   149
End Notes   153
Bibliography   159
Appendix   171
Books by D.A. Chadwick   181

About The Author   182

Third Printing, 2021
Copyright © 2021 by D.A. Chadwick

All rights reserved. No part of this book may be reproduced, stored in a retrieval system or transmitted in any form or by any means without the prior written permission of the publishers, except by a reviewer who may quote brief passages in a review to be printed in a newspaper, magazine or journal.
WordMerchant Publications
El Dorado, Kansas
© 2021 by D.A. Chadwick

ISBN- 978-0-578-91115-1
Ebook ISBN 978-1-0878-7515-6
BISAC: History / American West/True Crime
Deer Creek: The Murders of William H. Gibson and John S. Frazer
Printed in the United States of America

Cover by M Y Cover Design

No author writes fiction or nonfiction without help and encouragement. I would like to thank my late friend, Joyce Akins, for rambling all over Kansas doing research with me back when many documents were not online or even on microfilm. She helped with my fictional account of the case, Blatherskites, published twenty years ago. It was a daunting task.

Acknowledgements

I would like to thank Sarah St. John with the Kansas Historical Society and the staff at the New York Public Library for their assistance during Covid-19 restrictions.

Characters Involved in the Frazer and Gibson Murder Investigations

Characters Involved in the Frazer and Gibson Murder Investigations

1. **William Harrison Gibson**

    Born; 1840 Pope County Illinois Died: May 22, 1890 at the Central Hotel, Moline, KS

    Height 5'10, eyes blue, hair light, fair complexion. Farmer.

    Wife: Harriet Jackson Born: 1850 Died: 1947

    Civil War veteran. 13th Illinois Calvary, Company M. Enlisted December 21, 1863 as sergeant at Wool, Illinois (Camp Butler) and discharged at Pilot Knob, Missouri August 31, 1865 as 2nd Lt. Joined by Capt. Norris.

    Director of The First National Bank in Howard in 1890.

    Children:

    Joseph F. Gibson -1869 to 1953 married Rose E. James 1890 to 1982.

    Mahala Mary Gibson: Was with her father at hotel when he died. Married Ahrburg

    Richard (Dick) Gibson Born: July 14, 1874 in Moline, KS Died: February 13, 1960 Fort Gibson, OK

    Samuel H. Gibson

    Harriet Ellen Gibson Gibson

Major Charley Gibson,
Lillie May Gibson Died at eight months old
William Walter Gibson,
Edward Ernest Gibson
James Gibson
Occupation: Banker/cattleman. Would have been head cashier at Farmer's and Drover's Bank in Eureka. Came to Howard in April 1871.

2. **John Samuel Frazer**

Born: 10/24/1858 Richmond (Grape Grove, Ray County, Missouri. Died June 28, 1890 in Chautauqua County, Kansas
Parents: William Triplett and Sarah A. (Owen, Bellis) Frazer
Occupation: Businessman/cattleman. Single
*Invested heavily in real estate in Moline, Kansas-Frazer's Addition and bought up farm land at sheriff's auctions. Also stockholder in Howard State Bank. Owned 8000 acres with Gibson.
*Established a market for all grades of stock. Several hundred thousand dollars invested.
* 10/28/1889 withdrew from some partnerships to focus on cattle.
*Early spring 1890 bought first Texas herd and imported them to Kansas. Fenced off large plots of land that had been open for free grazing.
Siblings: Rebecca Jane Frazer (1853-1877) married Alonzo Penniston (1846-1931), Thomas Stephen Frazer (1860-1856), William Triplett Frazer Jr. (1867-1932) and Sarah Elizabeth Frazer (1855-1940) Married Henry Woodruff (1849-1930) in Ute Creek, Costilla, Colorado 12/31/1882. From Polk Township, Dekalb County, Missouri.
Sarah Ann "Sally" Owen Frazer

Born: August 6, 1823

Clark County, Kentucky, USA

Died: February 22, 1905 (aged 81)

Ray County, Missouri, USA

Sarah Ann Owen Bellis Frazer was the daughter of Sarah Ann Gordon and John Owen, both of Goochland County, VA. Her parents were married in Clark Co, Kentucky. Sarah's siblings were: David, Elizabeth (White), Jackson, John, James, Margaret (Ware), Katherine, Mary (Rout), Robert, Rebecca (LeFever) and Clarissa (Baber?).

She married Samuel Bellis (1815-1847) on Oct 14, 1841 (Ray County, MO) and had the following Bellis children: Isabelle Margaret (Leake), Mary Charlotte (Parrott), William McCrosky and James Jackson.

On Nov. 18, 1851, after the death of Samuel Bellis, she married William Triplett Frazer (1808-1891) and had the following Frazer children: Rebecca Jane (Penniston), Sarah Elizabeth (Woodruff), John Samuel, Thomas Stephen and William, Jr.

Isabelle Margaret Bellis Leake

Born: November 16, 1842

Orrick, Ray County, Missouri, USA

Died: May 12, 1919 (aged 76)

Margaret Isabell Bellis Leake was the daughter of Sarah Ann Owen and Samuel Bellis. Her siblings with the Bellis surname were: Mary Charlotte (Parrott), William McCrosky and James Jackson.

After her father died, her mother remarried Triplett Frazer. Margaret's half siblings were Frazers: Rebecca Jane, Sarah (Sally), John Samuel, Thomas Stephen and William Triplett, Jr.

Margaret married Walter Scott Leake in Ray County, Missouri on Sept. 25, 1858 when she was 15 years old. They had the following nine children: George Washington, Albert Adolphus, Samuel Walter (worked for Frazer in Kansas- moved after murder), Gustavus Leonadus, Minnie Cordelia (Farris, Miller), Mary Jane ("Mollie" Penniston), Florence Emma, Rufus Emmet and Otha Monroe.

Margaret spent her life in Ray County, Missouri. She and her husband are associated with the New Hope Primitive Baptist Church, the oldest church in Ray County, MO, as members and donating the land. She died of shock from a fractured hip.

3. **William Riley Best**

Born: 10/15/1839 Died: 05/12/1897 Blount County, TN.
Wife: Thersa Malissa Keen Born 05/25/1854. Died 12/21/1923. Filed widow's pension July 7, 1897.
Occupation: Carpenter
Civil War veteran. 5th Tennessee Infantry. Filed disability pension August 4, 1890. Had relatives in Moline area they visited at time of murders. Left right afterwards. Connection to local Best family not certain.

4. **William Riley Jones**

Born: unknown Died: 1930 in Wichita, Sedgwick County
Owned pasture where Frazer's body was found. Rode bank fixing fence and saw body in waist high pool floating face downing a cramped position. Sent a boy to tell men searching the pasture.

5. **Grissom brothers**

John Grissom Born: 1867 in Kentucky. Died: Unknown
Thomas Abraham Grissom Born: August 23, 1869 in Hopkins County, Kentucky. Died: July 3, 1947 in Oklahoma City. Two of the alleged assassins that lived with their parents,

Solomon and Emily Grissom in Chautauqua County, Kansas near murder scene.

6. **Roscoe Greer**

   Saw man on horseback around 9 am on Old Trail. Was at the Grissom place 9 am to noon that Saturday returning a hoe and planter.

7. **James Richard Burgess**

   Born: September 7, 1857 in Saganon, Illinois. Died: September 17, 1945 Missoula, Montana

   Wife Sarah Burgess, testified at 1896 hearing.

   Rested at Binn's cabin Saturday around 10 am. Lived in Binn House when working for Frazer and Gibson. Arrested in 1896 and tried for Frazer murder with Olney, Leckliter, New and Cox.

   Married. Wife related to Jerry Hutton. Frank Kimsey (Both arrested for murder) was Burgess' cousin. Charged for murder 1896.

8. **Lena C. Goodell**

   Born: March 27, 1863 in Edinboro, Erie County, Pennsylvania. Died: October 7, 1937 in Sedan, Chautauqua, Kansas

   Heard two strange wails between 9 am and 10 am Saturday June 28 in canyon. Father,

   John Woodworth Goodell (Goodell was on Frazer's coroner's jury).

9. **Dr. Caleb Boyer Sipple**

   Born: October 13, 1851 Delaware. Died: September 24, 1890 Chautauqua County, Kansas,

   Examined Frazer's body for autopsy.

10. **George E. Martin**

    Cashier at Moline Bank partly owned by Frazer. Went with

Thomas S. Frazer and Calvert in September to trace the path of the killers.

11. **Rev. William Clark Goodwin**

    Born: September 3, 1837 in New York. Died: May 12, 1913 in Moline, Kansas.

    Minister at Methodist Episcopal Church in Moline. Wrote memorial to Frazer. Served in the 92nd Regiment in New York.

12. **Solomon Jenkins Grissom and Emily Grissom**

    Solomon-Born: March 8, 1839 in Tennessee. Died: December 6, 1926 in Chelsea, Oklahoma.

    Emily-Born: May 30, 181838 in Hopkins County, Kentucky. Died: December 2, 1897 in Stroud, Oklahoma. John and Thomas lived at home at time of the murders.

13. **Alonzo Kilmer**

    Born: December 7, 1834 in New York. Died: June 24, 1908 in Burr Oak, Michigan.

    Saw Thomas Grissom in Sedan with his father. Said he was looking to sell crops and move away. Kilmer noticed blood on Thomas's left sleeve.

14. **Charles Harvey Sherwin**

    Born March 17, 1848 in Ayer's Cliff, Quebec, Canada. Died January 29, 1933 in Hanford, California

    Saw John Grissom on Tuesday 10 am in front of Ackerman's hardware store. He also saw the blood stain 2 inches long and 14 inch wide on Grissom's sleeve and drew the attention of Oran S. Sumner and Alonzo Kilmer to it.

15. **William Henry Aiken**

    Born June 9, 1850 in New Castle, Ohio. Died June 16, 1934 in Meridian, Idaho.

    Said that John Grissom changed his mind about going to

town that day, it was too hot. Grissom said that he could tell who two of the killers were. Claimed to be at a neighbor's house June 28 before the Frazer's murder where the woman there said that Gibson was dead and Frazer would not live long.

16. **Harry Ellsworth Turner**

    Born May 1866 in Indiana. Died 1930.

    Heard John Grissom tell McGreer that he could take authorities to the parties that he thought knew about the murders of Gibson and Frazer. Saw blood on John' shirt sleeve.

17. **Eli .C. Ackerman**

    Born: August 31, 1847 Died: February 26, 1931.

    Was present when Frazer's body was found and had been on the search party. He found Frazer's hat which had three stains on the crown where someone had grabbed it.

18. **Mrs. John Greer**

    Saw Gray pass her house June 28 between 9 am and 10 am heading toward Spring Creek.

19. **Dr. Franklin S. Olney**

    Born June 21, 1839 in Pennsylvania. Died December 28, 1897 in Howard, Kansas.

    Coroner for Gibson murder. Charged with poisoning U.A. Buckingham in State v. Walters, Mrs. Wilson and Olney. The victim had rat poison in his coffee. Gibson was thought to have drank poisoned lemonade. Olney found cause of death to be unknown and that corrosion in his esophagus occurred post mortem.

    1850-1860 - Lived, Harrison, Potter Co., PA

    1861 - M.D. degree, Winchester Medical College, Winchester, VA

    During Civil War - Pvt., Co. G, 46th Pennsylvania Infantry

1870 - Druggist, Eureka, Greenwood Co., KS
1880 - Practiced medicine, Elk Falls, Elk Co., KS
1890 Owned Drug/Pharmacy store in Howard, Kansas
1897- Owned Drug/Pharmacy store in Elk Falls, Kansas with Frank Shinn
12/28/1897 - Died, Howard, Elk Co., KS

20. **Marquis D "Marcus" "Mark" McBee**

    Born: August 9, 1861 in Tennessee. Died: December 30, 1927 in Oak Valley, Elk County.

    A druggist in Howard and one of those arrested for the death of Frazer in 1894. Was also charged with throwing eggs at the Salvation Army, but had a hung jury. Also reported the Elk courthouse burning in 1906 after his daughter first noticed it. He also carried general merchandise.

    Charged with murder in 1896 with Theo Cox, William Leckliter, John New, James Burgess and Franklin Olney.

21. **Elizabeth (Lizzie) Ruth Bryant**

    Born: November 23, 1868, in Louisburg Township Montgomery County. Died: November 11, 1941 in Elk City.

    Lived 14 miles west of Elk City (Oak Valley) on claim she won during the Oklahoma land rush of 1889 where she permanently crippled her foot. Graduated from college in Winfield and taught school in the Oklahoma Territory. She wore unusual clothes of a western style and helped the Dalton boys who later returned and aided Bryant in defending her claim. Friend of John Frazer.

    1885 lived in Longton, aged 17. September 27, 1887 married Issac Miles Watkins (born 1851 Jefferson, Indiana).

    Single in 1910 and 1920, widow in 1925 and 1930. In 1940 listed as divorced.

She lived primarily in Oak Valley, with brief time in Winfield.

22. **Christian Baker Leckliter**

Born: 12/29/1836 in Belmont County, Ohio Died: May 13,1906 in Howard, KS

Wife: Eliza Miller 10/01/1842 to 03/26/1909

Homesteaded three miles north of Howard in 1860. Sold farm in 1884 to open feed and grain store. Children: 7

William Harry- born in Howard, died in 1923 in Yorktown, Indiana.

John Steel-born in Howard, died in 1925 in San Francisco. Worked for the railroad.

Charles Christian- born 1871 in Howard, died in 1925 in Howard. Bought Dobyn's Hardware.

Grover- born 1877 in Howard, died in Oklahoma.

23. **Berndt Olson**

Born October 30, 1863 in Malma, Sweden. Died October 27, 1947.

Respected, but avoided due to his psychic abilities. He was a constable when Mace Gilbert was in court. Played cards with New, Best and Leckliter. Never accused of crime. Associate of Frazer and a farmer.

24. **Arthur Guy Logsdon**

Born: December 27, 1883 in Missouri. Died: 1925 in Rock Springs, Wyoming.

Time keeper. Lived on place Gibson managed and lost three cows to Tick Fever

25. **Charles Jackson**

Born: 1878 in Illinois. Died: Unknown

Brother of Harriet Jackson Gibson. Lost one cow to Tick Fever.

27. **Maude Hibbard**

Fashionable milliner in Moline that sold corsets, ladies wear etc., over Downing's store in Moline. Witness at 1896 trial.

30. Thomas Stephen Frazer

Brother of John Frazer from Ray County, Mo.
Born: September 6, 1860 Died: March 16, 1956
Came to the Elk County area to investigate brother's death.

31. Wesley Best (Captain)

Birthdate: October 19, 1827 Staunton, Macoupin County, Illinois. Lived in Litchfield, Illinois and Nashville before Kansas. Dark hair and eyes, swarthy complexion.

Kept ranch in Moline after moving to Columbus, Kansas where he spent winter of 1897. Returned to 122 or 118 N. Spruce, Nashville in 1897. Owned mill in Columbus with sons.

Death: June 28, 1904 Howard, Elk County, Kansas

Union army: Corporal, 46th Illinois Infantry, Company A 1861-1865. (Wesley J. Best). Mustered out as a private. Also a Wesley E. Best listed in naval service in 1877 stationed in Illinois.

Married 3 times: Mary Whittington, Martha Sawyer, Anna Burris White,
Children;

Burris C. Best (Ben) Born Feb 21, 1876 Married Ella Pendleton

Wesley E.: Born October 14, 1857 in Litchfield, Illinois. Married Lucy Gooch Hanson, November 1883. Died March 4, 1945 in Columbus, Kansas. Owned flour mill. Studied at University of Illinois for mining. Mine owner in Columbus in 1926.

Lillian: Born 1862 Litchfield, IL

Emma M: Born 1867 Died December 14, 1928 Seattle

Married James Herbert June 10, 1888, President of Cotton Belt Railroad

William G. Cutler's History of the State of Kansas

> WESLEY BEST & SONS, proprietors of the Excelsior Rolling Mills, established July; 1882. These mills form one of the grand manufacturing interests of Columbus. They are conducted upon the new roller process, are run by steam-power with a capacity of manufacturing 125 barrels of flour per day. The present dimensions are 30 x 58, with three stories and basement, but the enterprising managers, B. C. and W. E. Best (sons) propose enlarging considerably, not only upon the manufacturing capacities, but also enlarging extensively upon its present dimensions. They manufacture exclusively to the merchant trade, and are now turning out two excellent brands, the Patent and the Diamond. They are both practical mill men, having been reared to

the business in Alton, Ill., where the father still conducts an extensive business.

32. Sheriff Oley Richolson

Born: November 3, 1842 in Illinois. Died August 21, 1895, Buried at Elk Falls, Kansas

Farmer before elected sheriff. Appointed Deputy U.S. Marshall in August 1890. Parents from Norway

Married to Lizzie Richolson.

Four children, John, Nona, Amy and Ralph.

33. John W. Glenn

Born: November 27, 1839 in Indiana, Died: April 26, 1908, Sedan, Chautauqua County, KS.

Acquaintance and witness at inquest.

33. Jeremiah Hutton

Born" February 20, 1851 in Missouri. Died: June 24, 1923 in Kirk, Utah.

Suspect in murder of Frazer as fingered by amateur detectives Davis and West in 1892. Lived in Center Township.

34. S. Frank Kimsey

Accused by Davis and West of being one of the murderers. Lived Center Township, Chautauqua County.

35. Keenan Hurst

Born: March 5, 1839. Died: July 1, 1927, in Howard, Kansas

Member of the Kansas Livestock Commissioner's Board

Married to Margrete Lee Long. Four children, Wilber, Clara, Daniel and Lottye.

36. John Francis

Born: 1855 in Talkington, Illinois. Died: 1891 at Burden, Kansas. Buried in Girard, Crawford County, Kansas

Married to Jennie Summer Sept 4, 1883. She was granted a divorce October 7, 1891. Given custody of children and $1000 alimony. Elk County court. Children Aaron and Pearl.

Frazer's partner in the Long-Bell Company's Old Stand, Moline, Kansas. Bought cows and pigs for butcher, sold feed and coal. Later owned shop at A.W. Kelly building which he sold to D.C. and H.D. Brubaker in February 1891. Mayor of Moline in August 1888.

Owned meat market in Burden, Kansas December 1891. Sold coal at Vinson and McCaslin's hardware store in Moline 1885. Owned grocery store Colean and John's in Moline, 1889.

R. Quaterman- July, 20 1891 Sheriff's sale 13th district. Wife also included in suit.

37. Jacob Neinan Carr

Born: May 3, 1853 in Ohio. Died: 1930 in Sedan, Kansas.

Witness at preliminary hearing March 16, 1896 in Sedan.

38. Ellis Calvin McBrian

Born: March 24, 1849 Died: January 27, 1929 in Sedan.

Deputy under Sheriff Sandy Lowe in Chautauqua County 1890.

39. John Cleveland

Born: October 18, 1845. Died: January 13, 1907. Buried in Moline, Kansas.

Landlord of Palace Hotel and friend of John Frazer.

39. Daniel T. Barber

Born: October 19, 1858 in Bath Co., KY Died: Unknown

Worked at Grenola Livery in June 1890. Lived in Wild Cat Township in 1880. Returned to testify from Pawhuska, Oklahoma in 1896 hearing.

40. John W. Hanson (George)

Born: Unknown date in Illinois. Died: Unknown

Lived in Howard, Kansas

41. Daniel M. Woodworth

Born: April 15, 1845 Died: February 16, 1932 in Sedan, Kansas.

Name was originally, Glascow. Changed it after running away from home in 1859.

Post commander of Stones River, Kansas GAR 1923. Witness at 1896 trial. 1861 to 1864.

42. Campbell Smith Reed

Born 1862 in Kentucky. Prosecutor for Gibson/Frazer hearing March 16, 1896. Lived in Fredonia, Kansas

43. Dr. William H. Smethers

Born: February 20, 1851. Died: June 12, 1908 at Moline, Kansas.

Moline doctor acquainted with Dr. Olney and disagreed with autopsy results on Gibson. Had office at Whalings Drug Store in 1887.

44. Hiriam Sparks McCray

Born: November 30, 1849 in Hancock County, Indiana. Died: 1931 Fredonia, Wilson County, Kansas

Sheriff of Wilson County. New told his story about the murders to him when arrested.

45. Edgar Chill

Born: 1871 in Kansas. Died: Unknown

Lived in Sedan, Chautauqua, Kansas in 1880.

Rode fence for Sheriff Lowe 1890.

46. Fred (Freddy) Mack Loyd

Born: December 17, 1884. Died: 1936 Sedan, Chautauqua County, Kansas

12 year old who found the bloody knife near the pool. Harry Lloyd, his cousin with him.

47. Harvey Pierce Moser

Born: June 13, 1851 in Saline, Illinois. Died: January 20, 1924 in Livingston, Merced, California.

In January 1891 lived in Sedan, Chautauqua, Kansas, United States. County commissioner who told Davis they were hiring a Pinkerton detective to solve the case.

48. Dr. Milton Trowbridge Evans

Born: February 1859 in Illinois. Died: April 23, 1934.

Did inquest of Frazer in 1890. Testified at 1896 hearing in Sedan.

49. Dr. John M. Sharpless

Born: January 1845 in Ohio. Died: May 1914 in Texas.

Did inquest of Frazer in 1890. Testified at 1896 hearing in Sedan.

50. Ike Hudson

Postmaster of Fredonia, Kansas. Testified at 1896 hearing about John New's reputation.

51. C.M. Ellis

Justice of the Peace in Sedan. Civil War veteran. Kansas Calvary, Regiment 9, company B. Corporal.

52. Charles McKesson

Born: July 7, 1857 in Iowa. Died: March 15, 1925 in Los Angeles, California.

Chautauqua County D.A. during 1896 hearing.

53. Richard (Dick) Speed

Born September 8, 1831 in England. Died September 20, 1913 in Sedan, Kansas.

Lived in Center Township, Chautauqua County in 1890. Drummer in the Union army. 1st Kansas Regiment, Company D. Justice of the peace in Sedan. Small in stature. Known for years as "Uncle Dick".

Probate judge in Sedan named Richard Speed. Gibson estate administered by J.J. Addams.

Son Richard Speed Jr. Born 1867 and Died 1893. Rode with Burgess to collect money from Best.

54. Enos H. Stoneback

Born: 1855 Died: November 22, 1935.

Lived in Center Township, Chautauqua County in 1890. Farmer.

55. **Peter Ellis McGrew (Ellis)**

Born: December 22, 1869 in Grayson County, Kentucky Died: January 29, 1929 Utah, buried in Independence, Kansas. Married to Lilly McGreen (Father was Richard Speed).

Lived in Summit, Center Township, Chautauqua County in 1880. Testified that he owned a knife that was lost near the pool in Deer Creek.

Family also called to testify for defense; Lillie and Alice McGrew.

56. **Reuben Harrison Nichols**

Born: March 14, Martinsville, Clark County, Illinois 1841. Died: March 27, 1921 in Woodward, Oklahoma

.Company B, 2nd Illinois Artillery. Private

Prosecutor in 1890 and defense counsel in 1896 trial. Lived in Elk Falls, Kansas.
Served in the Civil War

Buried in Chanute, Kansas

Obit-

Judge R.H. Nichols died at his office in Woodward, last Sunday morning, at 1:30, of acute indigestion. He had been at Buffalo attending District Court and had returned home Saturday night. About 1:00 o'clock he called his law partner, S.M. Smith, saying he was very ill and asking that he come to the office and bring a doctor. Mr. Smith responded at once but all efforts were unavailing and death came at 1:30.

Reuben Harrison Nichols was a son of Clark and Phoebe Nichols and was born in Clark County, Illinois, March 14, 1841. When the Civil war broke out he enlisted in Battery B, 2nd Illinois Artillery, serving with distinction till 1864, when he became a member of Gen. Hancock's Veteran Reserve Corps, in which organization he served as a dispatch messenger, and to him were entrusted many messages, the delivery of which involved the utmost hazard. While in this service it was Mr. Nichols' privilege to carry a message to President Lincoln and he treasured his meeting with Lincoln as one of the great moments of his life.

After the war he studied law and in 1868 was admitted to the bar. The same year, on June 13th he was married to Miss Olive Moffitt. To this union two daughters were born.

Moving to Kansas, Judge Nichols established a large practice and was recognized as one of the best attorneys in the state, earning a reputation for square dealing and upright manhood that won recognition and he was elected in 1871 to the House of Representatives and in 1876 to the Kansas State Senate. He was an ardent advocate to temperance and while serving in the Kansas

Senate, introduced and put thru the amendment that made Kansas the first prohibition state in the Union.

About ten years ago Judge Nichols came to Woodward where he resided till his death, practicing law here, as where he had formerly lived, exemplifying in his life the highest principles of manhood and patriotism.

He was an orator of more than usual ability and was in demand for addresses on many occasions.

He was a member of the Methodist church, of the Masonic and Odd Fellow lodges and of the G.A.R.

He is survived by his wife and one daughter, Mrs. F.W. Sherwood, of Iola, Kansas.

Funeral services were conducted at Chenoweth's Parlors Monday afternoon, by his pastor, Rev. R.D. Pool, who paid tribute to the distinguished service the deceased had rendered and the beneficent influence of his life. The casket, draped with the Flag for whose protection he fought, was covered with flowers whose beauty and perfume were a token of the high esteem in which the deceased was held by friends and associates, whose sympathy is extended the bereaved family. The remains were shipped to Chanute, Kansas, Monday night for interment beside the daughter who died three years ago.

https://www.findagrave.com/memorial/61319209

57. Thomas Napoleon King

Born: Date unknown in Hart County, Kentucky. Died: October 1916 in Sedan, Kansas.

Defense counsel for 1896 trial.

Civil War veteran: Co. D 2nd Kentucky Cavalry

Enlistment Date: 24 Oct 1861

Side Served: Union.

58. Thomas Jefferson Hudson

Born: October 30, 1839. Died: January 4, 1923 in Wichita, Kansas

Defense counsel in 1896 trial. Lived in Fredonia and was mayor for years. US Congressman. Elected to represent Kansas' 3rd District in the United States House of Representatives, serving from 1893 to 1895.

59. Legrand B. McPheron

Testified at 1896 trial. Friend of Harriet Gibson.

60. John Lovitt

Testified at 1896 trial. Member of the W.H. Gibson GAR post.

61. Sandy Lowe

Born: August 12, 1829 in St. Louis County, Mo. Died: October 10, 1902, buried at Sedan, Kansas

7th Mo S M Cav 2nd Lt, enlisted as a private. Later a captain. Sheriff of Chautauqua County in 1890.

62. Archer Hammond

Born: November 12, 1832 in Tennessee Died: August 28, 1913 in Sedan, Kansas

A Civil War veteran, Stone River Post No. 74, G.A.R.

Archer Hammond was born at Russel, W.Va., Nov. 21, 1832. He moved from there to Missouri and in 1862 enlisted in Company E 4th regiment Vol Cavalry. He was wounded in the head in the battle of Big Blue River and left unattended on the battle field two days. All the subsequent years of his life he has been a sufferer from the wound. He was honorable discharged at St. Louis, April 16th, 1865.

Land was northeast of crime scene.

63. James M. Brown

Born: December 2, 1839 in Green City, Hickory, Missouri. Died July 13, 1913 in Jetmore, Hodgeman, Kansas.

Testified at 1896 trial. Lived half a mile west of the Gibson pasture.

64. Clarence Edwin Anderson

Lived at Colfax, Wilson County. Was with Brown June 18, 1890 when they saw Burgess

US Navy veteran.

65. Willis Edmund (Bud) Baker

Born September 30, 1872 in Carrollton, Carroll, Missouri. March 27, 1961 in Pawhuska, Osage, Oklahoma.

Was with Brown June 18, 1890 when they saw Burgess.

66. Henry Oliver

Born: February 9, 1872 in Illinois. Died: May 18, 1954 in Cedar Vale, Chautauqua County, Kansas.

Booking agent.

67. Richard S. Blair

Born: Circa 1852 in Indiana. Died: Unknown

Lived in Howard, Kansas. Countered New's testimony about McBee and the Coxes being in Grenola June 27, 1890.

68. Stephen Arthur Mahurin

Born: March 17, 1870 in Howard, Elk, Kansas. Died: September 30, 1945 in Los Angeles, California.

69. George Washington Satterlee

Born: February 16, 1852 near Morris, Illinois. Died: September 16, 1911 in Center Township, Chautauqua, Kansas

Richard Gibson stayed at his house June 17, 1890 on the Gibson Grenola Road. Testified that he saw five riders heading toward the Gibson school house.

70. **William Henry Downing**

Born: September 22, 1856 in Mazeppa, Wabasha, Minnesota. Died: March 24, 1890 in Moline, Elk, Kansas.

Became a partner with John Frazer in the Moline Store and the Moline Bank in 1885.

71. **Albert B. Good,**

Born: December 1855 in Warren, Huntington, Indiana. Died: October 15, 1916 in Fresno, California.

On coroner's jury for William Gibson May 1890.

72. **Edward M Shearer**

Born: September 8, 1847 in Randolph County, Indiana. Died: June 20, 1916 in Sapulpa, Creek, Oklahoma.

On coroner's jury for William Gibson May 1890.

73. **Dr. William H Mason**

Born: April 18, 1841 Died: June 22, 1900 in Ottawa, Franklin County, Kansas.

On coroner's jury for William Gibson May 1890.

74. **Joseph G. Debenbrink**

Born: September 19, 1855 in Lafayette County, Missouri. Died: July 7, 1935 in Savannah, Andrew, Missouri.

Postmaster of Wauneta, Chautauqua County in 1893.

Interviewed at Frazer's inquest June 1890. Identified body.

75. **Allen A. Wilson**

Born: November 2, 1853 in Indiana. Died: August 31, 1899 in Sedan, Kansas

Chautauqua County deputy under Hartzell. Arrested John H. Cox, Mark McBee and Wesley Best in 1894.

City Marshal Bud Wilson was shot and killed and a Chautauqua County Deputy Sheriff was badly wounded by two cousins they attempted to arrest on a warrant for horse stealing in Missouri. A posse apprehended both suspects four days later. Marshal Wilson was survived by his wife and seven children.

https://www.findagrave.com/memorial/23349131/allen-a_-wilson.

76. **Daniel Stough**

Born: Unknown Died: July 29, 1915 in Sedan, Kansas.

Civil War veteran. Company E 126 Illinois Infantry Volunteers. Also Company D, Illinois Regiment 121

Chautauqua County deputy under Hartzell. Arrested John H. Cox, Mark McBee and Wesley Best in 1894.

Sedan postmaster in 1906-1910.

77. **William F. Steadman**

Born: October 1854 in Boston, Massachusetts Died: Unknown.

Chautauqua County deputy under Hartzell. Arrested John H. Cox, Mark McBee and Wesley Best in 1894.

Daughter Minnie Glover was murdered by gun shot in San Antonio, Texas November 2, 1917.

78. **Samuel Treville Hartzell (Hartsel)**

Born: January 22, 1851 in Franklin, Des Moines, Iowa. Died: March 7, 1927 in Des Moines County, Iowa.

Chautauqua County Sheriff 1894. Arrested John H. Cox, Mark McBee and Wesley Best.

79. **Charles L. Lane**

Born: June 13, 1857 in Zanesville, Ohio. Died: June 27, 1931 in Modesto, Stanislaus County, California.

Partner of Wesley Best in selling Herefords. Lived in Moline in 1885. Stock buyer and veterinarian in Coffeyville, Kansas and Newkirk, Oklahoma in 1900.

80. **Joseph Marion Johns**

Born: in October 31, 1853 in Illinois. Died: November 27, 1834 in Moline, Kansas.

Partner with John Colean in feed/stock store in Moline. Owned creamery in 1920.

81. **William W. Littel**

Born: July 24, 1843 in Harrison, Indiana. Died: July 24, 1925 in Caney, Montgomery, Kansas.

Lived in Center Township in 1890. Testified at 1896 trial.

82. **Oliver G. Kiser**

Born: 1860 Died: Unknown.

Sheriff of Chautauqua County in 1896. Lived in Lafayette, Kansas.

83. **Abe Harris**

Inmate at Leavenworth February 19, 1906

Witness at 1896 trial. Lived in Lafayette, Chautauqua County in 1890.

84. **John M. Cooper**

Witness for defense for John New. Lived in Neodesha.

85. **Clark Solomon Wicks**

Witness in 1896 trial. Lived in Fredonia in 1896. Civil War veteran. Member of Phil Harvey Post 89.

86. Susan H. Williams

Witness for defense in 1896 trial. Lived in Summit, Chautauqua County in 1896.

87. William T. Kimzey (Kimsey)

Born: Oct 1869 in Dallas, St. Clair, Mo. Died: Aug 11, 1944 Oak Valley, Elk, Kansas.

Witness in 1896 trial. Lived in Center, Chautauqua County in 1885.

88. John Denton

Witness for 1896 trial.

89. William M. Dory Jr. (Dorge)

Born: August 26, 1856 in New York. Died: May 29, 1941 in Grenola, Kansas.
Witness for 1896 trial.

90. James Fletcher

Witness for 1896 trial. Lived in Lafayette, Chautauqua County in 1890.

91. R.W. M. Roe

Witness for 1896 trial. Lived in Grenola and Howard, Kansas.

92. Mrs. Murphy

Witness in 1896 trial. Lived in Thayer, Kansas.

93. Dr. James P. Graham

Died: 1899 in Chautauqua County.
State witness at 1896 trial. Was at Frazer inquest.

94. L. Flagler (Flaglin)

On witness list for 1896 trial.

95. John and Kate Kiefson

Witnesses at 1896 trial.

96. Walter A. McCausland

Born: 1859. Died: 1921 in Hollister, California.
Witness at 1896 trial. Listed as law student in 1888. Lived in Howard, Kansas in 1895.

97. J. G. Marshall

Witness at 1896 trial. Lived in Neosho County, Kansas.

98. F. Schoffen (Schaffen)

Witness at 1896 trial. Druggist in Howard.

99. Joseph Henry Glascock

Born: July 3, 1865 in Rock Island County, Illinois. Died: January 29, 1960 in Elk Falls, Kansas. Died in a fire. Buried at Moline, Kansas.
Witness at 1896 trial.

100. **Alexander Frank McCaslin (Frank)**

Born: October 1, 1850 • Monroe County, Tennessee. Died: November 8, 1921 • Emporia, Lyon County, Kansas, USA
Witness at 1896 trial. Owned hardware store in Moline 1885.

101. **Daniel M. Ellis**

Witness at 1896 trial. Lived at Wild Cat, Elk County 1880. Farmer.

102. **John M. Harris**

Witness at 1896 trial.

103. **Michael H. Hanlon**

Born: 1850. Died: 1896 in Caney, Montgomery County, Kansas.
Witness at 1896 trial.

104. **Florence Hamilton (Mcbride)**

Born November 18, 1874 in Washington County, Illinois. Died May 17, 1904 in Howard, Elk County, Kansas.
Witness at 1896 trial.

105. **Thomas P. Wynn and Minnie Wynn**

Father and daughter.
Witnesses at 1896 trial. Father was employee of Wesley Best.

106. **William Doolin**

Witness at 1896 trial. Lived at Cedar Vale, Kansas. Civil War veteran.

107. **Everett E. Turner**

Born: October 26, 1861. Died: August 30, 1946 in Hewins, Kansas. Jury member in 1896 trial.

108. **James W. Uhls James Reynolds, Everett E. Turner, Samuel G. Shirk, Iain N. Drake, Charles A. Dale, John Wilkinson, John Chittendon, David Franklin Arbaugh, James Tolson Botts, and J.W. Laverly.**

Jury members for 1896 State vs Burgess trial at Sedan.

109. **Judge A. M. Jackson**

Born: 1860 in Kentucky.
Judge at 1896 trial of Burgess in Sedan. Lived in Howard, Kansas in 1885.

110. **John Henry Cox**

Born: February 15, 1849 in Rushsylvania, Logan, Ohio. Died: January 4, 1938 in Howard, KS.

Arrested with McBee and Best in 1894. Called as witness for defense in 1896 by Scott.

112. James J. Hamilton

Witness for defense at 1896 trial. Lived in Elk County. Died in 1898.

113. Ulysses Grant Way (Grant)

Born: 1863 in Winchester, Randolph County, Indiana. Died: August 1912 in Independence, Montgomery County, Kansas.

Witness for Defense in 1896 trial.

114. William Clement Foreman

Born: December 28, 1849 in Springfield, Sangamon County, Illinois. Died: December 16, 1931 in Independence, Montgomery County, Kansas.

Witness for Defense in 1896 hearing.

115. Philip Gephart

Born: May 17, 1851 in Sandusky County, Ohio. Died: November 23, 1916 Independence, Montgomery County, Kansas.

Witness for Defense in 1896 hearing.

116. Robert Swain

On witness list for 1896 trial.

117. Frank Atherton

Born: February 6, 1861. Died: June 2, 1940 in Dexter, Cowley County, Kansas.

Witness for the Defense in 1896 hearing.

118. G.M. Atherton

Witness for the Defense in 1896 hearing. Carpenter in Howard in 1888.

119. Frederick New

Union Center South Half Elk County, Kansas. Farmer.

Witness for the Defense in 1896 hearing

120. Sam Berry

Witness for State in 1896 trial. Lived in Howard.

121. John Vance Hammel

Born: March 8, 1866 in Wyandotte, Kansas. Died: March 13, 1932 in Grenola, Kansas.

Witness for State in 1896 trial.

122. Thomas J. Mitchell

Born: May 3, 1847. Died: May 3, 1914 in Howard, Kansas.

Lived in Howard, Kansas. Civil War veteran. Private, Company N, Regiment 15. Contacted heart disease in service.

Witness for State in 1896 trial.

123. Jake Campbell

Witness for State in 1896 trial. Farmer.

124. **Nancy J. Martin**

Witness for State in 1896 trial.
Lived in Elk Falls, Kansas.

125. **W. D.H. Shockey**

Born: Unknown date in Fenny County, Kentucky. Lived in Elk Falls and Shockey, Kansas. Civil War veteran, private, 45th Kentucky Volunteer Infantry. Farmer.
Witness for State in 1896 trial.

126. **Eli Sanborn**

Born: January 1, 1857 in Missouri. Died: December 17, 1932 in Cedar Vale, Kansas.
Witness for State in 1896 trial. Farmer.

127. **G.R. Wallace**

Witness for State in 1896 trial. Farmer. Lived in Elk County in 1888.

128. **James Edward (Ed) Lambert**

Born: November 1862 in Shelbyville, Shelby, Illinois. Died: 1918 in Chautauqua, Chautauqua, Kansas.
Witness for State in 1896 trial.

129. **George Bales**

Witness for State in 1896 trial.

130. **R.H. Ellworth**

Witness for State in 1896 trial.

131. **Mrs. A.C. Nye**

Witness for State in 1896 trial.
Lived in Spring Creek, Cowley County. Husband was a stockman.

132. **Lauren E. McSpadden**

Born: December 3, 1863. Died: October 14, 1920 in Sedan, Kansas.
Witness for State in 1896 trial.

133. **Oscar Benton Good**

Born: May 1850 in Green County, Illinois. Died: February 14, 1939 in Chautauqua, Chautauqua County, Kansas. Lived in Sedan and Summit, Kansas.
Witness for State in 1896 trial.

134. **Cyrus Benton Bendeur (Bendure)**

Born: November 1862 in Indiana. Farmer. Lived in Wild Cat Creek, Elk County, Kansas.
and Florence Black Bendeur

Born: June 16, 1856 in Donnellson, Montgomery County, Illinois. Died February 1, 1943 in Mound Valley, Labette County, Kansas.

Witnesses for State in 1896 trial.

135. **T.A. Middleston**

Witness for State in 1896 trial.

136. **Mrs. John F. New (Alice Wilson New)**

Wife of John New and witness for State in 1896 trial.

137. **John Fredrick New**

Born: March 27, 1856 in Illinois. Died: June 12, 1932 in Lexington, Lafayette County, Missouri.

Confession started the 1894 and 1896 hearing and trials. Lived in Fredonia in 1896. Worked as brick mason in Colorado.

138. **F.M. Marlin**

Witness for State in 1896 trial.

139. **Aaron Clum**

Born: March 14 1840 in Milford, Michigan. Died: in July 22, 1897 in Eureka Springs, Arkansas.

Witness for State in 1896 trial. Lived near Howard, Kansas in 1890.

140. **John S. Kane**

Witness for State in 1896 trial.

Telegraph operator from Howard in 1894 and a long time prior. Agent for Topeka, Atchison and Santa Fe Railroad Company and telegraph operator for Western Union. Stated that all correspondence he sent was destroyed as required during that period and no copies of messages were made.

141. **W. G. Wells**

Telegraph operator from Lansing in 1896. Western Union telegraph operator for Topeka, Atchison and Santa Fe Railroad Company in August and September 1896. Stated that all correspondence he sent was destroyed as required during that period and no copies of messages were made.

142. **List of 42 names from petition for change of venue petition to prove prejudice.**

John James Harmon Sedan Born November 11, 1849 in Indiana. Died 11/24/1936 in Sedan.

E.H. Richards and son Sedan

John T. Parman Sedan Born 1/25/1869 in Missouri. Died 3/15/1950 in Chautauqua.

James Hammer Ruddle Born 6/8/1843 in Branch, Virginia. Died 1/21/1921 in Moline.

O.A. Ruddle
Homan A. Ruddle Layfette. Born May 1879 in Virginia. Died 1915.
William P. Downard Elk City Born 11/5/1839 in Warren, Ohio. Died 1/7/1904 in Elk City.
R.J. Johnson
John B. Hunter
John A
Wallace Cerdidt
Henry Walters Layfette.
W.A. Laukely
J.L. Cefford
L.W. Walker
William Benduring
S.J. Githens
C.H. Clam
John Harlin Lawson Hendricks, Chautauqua County.
Samuel Donaldson
A.H. Beard
E.C. McBrian
Harvey Jamison
B.A. Leheun
H.R. Thompson
H. Sharver
E.U. Herton
J.W. Swiney
J.C. Scott
F.M. Conner
D.H. Pyles
A. Donahue
W.H. Crum
J.L. Patterson
W.M. Jordan
Heinz Burns
W.G. Holsten
Hiram Ager
W.W. Gilstrap
J.W. Landsdown
Samuel Donelson from Sedan. Died in 1918
[Some names illegible]

143. H. G. Mosier

Born: 1873 in Ohio.

Mentioned as agitator during 1894 hearing by R.H. Nichols when filing change of venue in 1896.

Lived in Wauneta. Residence in 1895 Fairview, Butler County. Residence in 1905 Topeka, Shawnee County.

144. Thomas B. Turner

Born 1848 in Tennessee. Died June 7, 1922.

Witness sought by the State in 1896 trial in Oklahoma Territory. Lived in Jefferson, Chautauqua County in 1939. Lived in Howard, Elk County Kansas in 1873 and bought 160 acres in Chautauqua County.

Civil War veteran. 51st Missouri Infantry, Company C.

145. Auborn Family

Witnesses sought by the State in 1896 trial in Oklahoma Territory.

146. John Edward Brogan

Born: August 15, 1845 in Madrid, St Lawrence, New York. Died: July 28, 1926 in Moline, Elk, Kansas.

Paid $1000 of Theo Cox's bail for 1896 Greenwood trial. Farmer. Veteran at Fort Riley.

147. Samuel Donelson

Paid $1000 of Mark McBee's bail for 1896 Greenwood trial.

148. Theodore Frelinghuzen Cox

Born: May 18, 1851 in Rushsylvania, Logan, Ohio. Died: March 4, 1939 in Howard, Elk, Kansas.

Charged and tried for Frazer murder in 1896. Arrested in 1894 with brothers John and Elmer Cox.

Blacksmith in Howard.

149. Elmer Ellsworth Cox

Born: March 1861 in Rushsylvania, Logan, Ohio. Died: 1942 in Kansas.

Arrested in 1894 with brothers John and Theo Cox. Tinner.

150. John Woodworth Goodell

Born: August 22, 1833 in Edinboro, Erie, Pennsylvania. Died: January 5, 1907 in Sedan, Chautauqua, Kansas.

Daughter Lena heard screams from Hunter's Canyon Saturday June 28, 1890. He served on the Frazer coroner's jury.

151. Charles M. Weber

Assistant Superintendent for Pinkerton's at Kansas City station.

152. Frank F. Hendricks

Born: 1862 Died: February 1896

Discovered coat and vest of John Frazer 250 yards from pool where body was found. Was with Silas Walker.

153. Silas Edward Walker

Born: October 26, 1856 in Illinois. Died: October 31, 1931 in Vinita, Oklahoma. Lived in Sedan. Blacksmith.

Discovered coat and vest of John Frazer 250 yards from pool where body was found. Was with Frank Hendricks.

154. Walter. S. Lambert

Born: 1859. Died: Unknown.

Loan officer from Moline, establishing the new Farmers' and Drover's Bank at Eureka where Gibson would be the head cashier. Traveled on train from Eureka with Gibson day before he died.

155. John P. Thomas Davis

Born: 1860 in Wabash, Wabash, Indiana. Died: 1939 in Sedan, Chautauqua, Kansas.

Lived in Sedan. Amateur detective who claimed to have solved the murders and sold an article to the Kansas City Journal in August 1892 leading to the arrests of Frank Kinsey and Jerry Hutton. Also sent it to the New York Press which published it between 1891 and August 1892.

156. Samuel N. West

Born: 1862 in Pennsylvania. Died: Unknown date in Kansas City, Missouri.

Amateur detective who sought reward money along with partner, Davis. Farmer and stockman.

157. Daniel M. Pile

Born: March 21, 1858 in McDonough County, Illinois. Died: June 8, 1895 in Chautauqua County, Kansas.

Wrote letter to the editor of The Advocate in Topeka to discredit the article in The Kansas City Journal on September 2, 1892.

158. Lewis Hanback

Born: March 27, 1839 in Scott County, Illinois. Died: September 7, 1897 in Topeka, Kansas

Sent by Governor Humphrey to investigate Frazer murder in response to rumors of political motivations.

United States Congressman. He served in the United States House of Representatives as a Republican from the 6th Congressional District of the State of Kansas in the Forty-eighth and Forty-ninth Congresses from March 4, 1883 to March 3, 1887.

159. William Henry Potter

Born: February 13, 1869 in Missouri. Died: January 15, 1950 in Oklahoma.
On coroner's jury for William Gibson May 1890.

160. A.F. McCaslin

On coroner's jury for William Gibson May 1890.

161. Dr. H.N. Mason

On coroner's jury for William Gibson May 1890.

162. William E. White (Bill)

Born: 1860 in Wisconsin.
Merchant and colleague of Frazer. Lived on Kansas Avenue in Longton 1900. Rode with Frazer from Kansas City to Moline June 14th before discovering effects of Tick Fever.

163. James Webb

Farmer and colleague of Frazer. Rode with Frazer from Kansas City to Moline June 14th before discovering effects of Tick Fever. Lived in Wild Cat, Elk County 1880.

164. John King Glasscock

Born: December 1832 in Ohio. Died: August 18, 1912 in Moline, Elk, Kansas
Lawyer, land agent, real estate loans in Moline. Included in Sheriff subpoenas.

165. Samuel Walter Leake

Born: September 5, 1864 in Richmond, Ray County, Missouri. Died: April 7, 1929 in Dixonville, Oregon.
Worked for Frazer and saw him that Friday morning. Described his clothing at inquest and habit of carrying a check book and gold watch. He was Frazer's nephew. Moved to Oregon in 1890.

166. Enos Bell Munday

Born: September 18, 1854 in Glascow, Illinois. Died: October 8, 1932 in Cedarvale, Kansas
Witness in 1890 for Frazer being missing. Saw Frazer that morning. An acquaintance of Frazer's.

167. William R. Hillman

Born: 1836 in Indiana. Died: July 2, 1897 in Sedan, Kansas
Witness at preliminary hearings in 1890. Saw John Grissom in Sedan with blood stain on his shirt.

168. C. Van Haines

Witness for John and Tom Grissom in 1890 preliminary hearings. Lived in Liberty and Oak Valley, Elk County.

169. Captain Sandy Lowe

Born: August 12, 1828 St. Louis County, Missouri. Died: October 10, 1902 in Sedan, Chautauqua County, Kansas.

Sheriff of Chautauqua County at time of Frazer murder.

Civil War veteran D Cass Co. Mo. H. Gd Cavalry; A; G 7 Mo. S. M. Cavalry.

170. John Francis Colean

Born: 1855 in Madison County, Illinois. Died: 1891 in Burden, Kansas. Buried in Girard, KS.

In business with Frazer in the Moline Feed store.

Wife granted a divorce in 1891 with custody of children. Death under mysterious circumstances.

171. John George Mullendore

Born: Unknown Died: .July 1907

Shareholder of Howard State Bank in 1890 along with John Frazer.

In cattle business with Lambert, also a shareholder.

Chosen to attend Democratic Convention in Wichita August 20, 1890.

172. George D. Hoy

Born: September 1840 in Ohio County, Indiana. Died: November 14, 1913 in Kay County, Oklahoma.

Auctioneer for Gibson estate.

173. John Downing McBrian

Born: September 10, 1840 in Mount Vernon, Illinois. Died: March 20, 1921 in Sedan, Kansas.

Attorney for Gibson estate. Also a minister. Chaplain at Lansing for eight years. A freemason as many in the area.

174. Edgar (Eddy) Harris

Born: March 29, 1871 in North Carolina. Died: Commerce, Oklahoma.

Porter who escorted Gibson to his hotel room in Moline, Kansas.

Lived in Galena, Kansas in 1900. Eventually owned a grocery store there. Married Louvina Dockery in May 1894.

175. Henry Deloice Means

Born: September 10, 1869 in Woodburn, Iowa. Died: December 13, 1935 in Burlington, Kansas.

176. Thomas Jefferson Hudson

Born: October 13, 1839 in Jamestown, Indiana. Died: January 4, 1923 in Wichita, Kansas.

Defense council.

176. Presley Hale Gallion

Born July 1847 in Jackson, Indiana. Died September 12, 1924 in Riverside County, CA.
Civil War veteran. Private in Indiana Volunteer Infantry 118, Company L.
Lived in Moline, Kansas in 1890 and wrote letters regarding the murders to the Moline Republican. Ran for Register of Deeds.

177. **William White**

Born November 8, 1844 in Iowa. Died September 13, 1931 in Moline, Kansas.
Associate cattleman of John Frazer. Made trips to Kansas City with him.

178. **John James Webb**

Born April 30, 1851 in Devizes, Wiltshire, England. Died September 7, 1933 in Howard, Elk, Kansas.
Associate cattleman of John Frazer. Made trips to Kansas City with him.

179 **Charles M. Luther McKesson**

Born June 7, 1857 in Iowa. Died March 15, 1925 in Glendale, California.
Elk County District Attorney in 1890 investigations and 1894.

180. **Senator Snyder Solomon Kirkpatrick**

Born: February 21, 1848 in Franklin, Illinois. Died: April 5, 1909 in Fredonia, Kansas.
Assisted in investigation of Frazer murder with Prosecutor McGuire in 1892.

Prologue

"It is the blatherskites who are the least hurt who most generally do the most squealing"
Moline Republican July 11, 1890

June 28, 1890 Chautauqua County, Kansas

The following tale with various alterations is one known to many whose ancestors lived in Elk and Chautauqua Counties in the nineteen century. The author also heard the story growing up including the added information that nine men were involved in the stabbing death of Frazer and each one took a turn inserting the blade, so that all would share the blame. Dozens of men were arrested for the crime of killing Frazer and his partner, William Gibson, but in the end no one was convicted. The murders remain unsolved, but not from a lack of effort on the part of law enforcement or the court system. The author's third great grandfather, Andrew Daniel Lawless, was in the Elk and Chautauqua County areas for the land rush of 1889 and may well have known John Frazer as Lawless was also a cattle owner in Wisconsin. He applied for his Civil War pension from Woodson County, Kansas in 1890. The following story is reprinted from a fictionalized book, *Blatherskites*, written by the author in 2000.

A Legendary Tale

It was apparent even by eight in the morning that the day would be humid and miserably hot. The Kansas sun was barely off the horizon, but already John S. Frazer could feel the moisture from his armpits begin to soak the blue-striped cotton shirt beneath his light gray coat. He removed his gray wool hat to wipe the sweat from his forehead. His mother, Sarah, had told him many times that a businessman should also be a gentleman which meant wearing suit coats and vests when a man in shirt sleeves could pass out from the heat. But soon, he would be able to go home and relax.

Frazer was exhausted from fatigue and worry. He had gone without sleep since he had stepped from the train at Moline last Tuesday morning. How had things gone to hell so rapidly? Frazer spent Monday the June 23, 1890 shipping cattle back east to a slaughter house at a good profit. The train ride from Kansas City to Moline had been pleasant enough for John and his fellow stockmen, Bill White and James Webb. John, who was basically a loner, had even socialized with other passengers and told a few jokes because he had been in such a light-hearted mood.

The market for Texas cattle seemed to have unlimited room for expansion and Frazer especially enjoyed handling stock. He had recently sold his share in The Moline Store back to Downing so that he could concentrate his efforts in livestock. Just five days earlier it had seemed like the world had nothing but goodness to offer. Then he heard the rumors while still standing at the Moline depot. Cattle were dropping dead all over Elk and Chautauqua counties from Spanish Fever that was brought from Texas in the Longhorn cattle of Frazer and Gibson. While it was true that he traveled often, Frazer had been back home frequently and would have seen the damage himself. He was shocked at the news.

John remembered the sick feeling in his stomach when his friend, Lizzie Bryant, had told him that she feared for his continued good health. She had not actually seen any of the dead cattle, but had heard of the note left on a fence post suggesting that Frazer would meet the same fate as Gibson if he remained in Kansas. If Elizabeth Bryant was scared, then there was a real problem. The woman had taught school in the Oklahoma territory and made plans to have land of her own in Elk County. She was the rebellious type and a pioneer who would go against the grain do what was right. The look in her eyes told Frazer that he could very well have the same fate as William Gibson who had died just one month earlier.

The coroner's jury found the cause of death to be unknown, but most everyone in Moline thought that Gibson had drank lemonade laced with rat poison. Dr. Olney had dismissed the corrosion in Gibson's esophagus as postmortem activity, but many had serious doubts. Frazer could not imagine that his partner's death was natural either, but at the time John didn't really believe anyone else would be killed. It was disturbing that Olney had once been charged with poisoning the coffee of one U.A. Buckingham only a few months earlier, but the case had been dismissed.

John W. Glenn waved to Frazer as he rode the gentle black mare past his farm. The man offered him a drink from his well, but John declined. He would take a rest and get a drink from the spring in Hunter's canyon a few miles away. Since last Tuesday Frazer had written many checks to those who claimed losses due to his Texas cattle and he still had two blank bank notes to sign.

It was almost over. The last few days had been nerve wracking, but John still believed in the basic goodness and reliability of his fellow citizens. Men could be reasoned with and compromises arranged without violence, though he was very aware that some did not like men such as Frazer who bought up land and fenced it off. There were many in the area that still believed in the free land, free water and free air philosophy. It was a difficult situation that had erupted to the point that John's friends and family had tried to persuade him to carry a revolver, but he refused. These men were his neighbors and were merely upset due to monetary loss. Frazer could make up for that type of loss and he had been doing just that for two days now.

It was nine o'clock when John Frazer nudged his horse through the gate that led to the old trail through Hunter's canyon. He was headed south to one of Gibson's pastures to check on the cattle there. So far, Frazer had found no disease in any of their Texas cattle. The trail ran through two steep hills. John W. Goodell's farm was to the east and Deer Creek School to the west. The creek passed through the grassy valley parallel to the trail, but was not running. It was a narrow stream that stood in isolated pools for most of the summer. A natural spring was just a few feet to the west of the trail. Horse and rider saw the cool water in the same instant and the animal picked up pace. "Good Girl, you've earned a drink." He patted the mare's neck.

As Frazer brought the horse up close to the spring, he saw two local brothers get up from their places on the ground. He tipped his hat and was about to ask about their families when he felt a sharp pain in his groin. The cut burned as he was pulled out of the saddle. A severe blow was dealt to the back of his head and John struggled to maintain a conscious state. His vision blurred, but he could make out several men before him. Two others held his arms tightly while one of the men walked up to spit in his face then stabbed him in his abdomen. Frazer let out a wail that shocked his attackers for a moment.

"You were warned, Goddamn it!" The man growled who had stabbed him. He pulled the knife out of Frazer's innards.

"Please, don't kill me! What else can I do? I paid you!" John wished that he could put some pressure on the wound that seeped into his vest. The pain was unbearable.

"You aren't wanted here, you Missoura scum." Another of the men took the knife and swung it at Frazer's body like he was cutting wheat. The blade was hooked and extremely sharp. Frazer screamed for help.

"Ain't nobody round here gonna help you." A voiced mocked him.

"For God sakes! Finish the son-of-a- bitch before he has half the county down here!" Remarked someone whom Frazer couldn't quite make out, but the voice was familiar.

Tears ran down the injured man's face from pain and fear. Could no one hear him? Frazer wondered as he felt the blade being placed against his throat. The blade bit into his neck and opened his jugular vein, sending a crimson tide down the front of the coat and vest.

"Jesus Christ! He's bleeding like a stuck pig. Oh God, it's all over me." Someone complained as John Frazer's head fell to his chest.

Frazer's sternum crackedas the blade penetrated it. A hand twisted the knife back and forth, shredding the stockman's cardiac muscle. "Should have gotten the hell outta here when you had the chance!" Rough laughter came from behind the dead man who was still being supported by his killers.

"Guess his HEART wasn't in it." Several of the men laughed.

Four of the assailants carried Frazer's lifeless body across the trail and tossed it some five feet from the path into knee high weeds. Another man approached with Frazer's fine wool hat in his bloody hand and dropped it near the owner.

"We'll take care of this later, somebody might have heard him bellow . . . Now go on, get out outta here."

The next afternoon the Grissom brothers returned to the scene to find the body coming out of rigor and flies were crawling all over it. While filling the air with curses, the two husky farm boys carried the body south to the hedge row that framed Arch Hammond's place then dragged the body through the brush and across the field to Jones' pasture where they followed Deer Creek.

When they came to a thicket of trees, the creek widened to a waist high pool. John Grissom hurriedly removed the coat, vest, watch and leather pocketbook from the dead man then they swung him, face down, into the water. It would not be long before someone found Frazer as the pool was a favorite swimming hole for local children and Hammond's damned dogs had already begun to howl at the scent of blood.

So goes the local legends passed down through the decades. The following book chronicles the law enforcement investigations and legal actions in the murders of John S. Frazer and his partner, William H. Gibson in 1890 Kansas.

One

History of Howard, Elk and Chautauqua Counties

L. J. Johnson of Tuscarawas County, Ohio came to Elk Falls, Kansas in 1869 and organized a petition to establish Howard County that winter. Trained as a surveyor he was awarded the contract to survey the county in 1870, which commenced in the fall of 1870 and finished in April, 1871. Johnson settled on Sections 2 and 3, Town 31, Range 11, which included the water-power of Elk Falls, an impressive waterfall of nine feet inspiring the town name. Not long after Johnson started a company with E. A. Hall, building the first mill in Howard County, three-stories high, with three buhr-stones in 1875. In 1872 he was elected County Surveyor of Howard County and in 1881 was elected surveyor of Elk County.[1]

Elk and Chautauqua counties were formed from Howard County in 1875. It was a division fiercely fought by local ranchers such as F. N. Hannant until Representative Edward Jaquins was elected and brought the separation bill before the house in 1874 where it passed in 1875. Hannant, a Civil War veteran and former POW at Libby Prison, owned thirty-five head of cattle. Another source of conflict for Howard County was the county seat war between Elk Falls and the town of Boston. When the governor signed a petition making Elk Falls the temporary county seat, feathers were ruffled. There was an election after that in which Boston won, but the corruption was so rampant that Judge Campbell invalidated the vote. It was also said that to win votes the people of Boston took turns filling the town well at night so that no one would know of its lack of a water supply. Boston perched on a hill some distance from a creek below requiring extensive effort to keep the well filled. No town could win the county seat without a water supply.

Shortly after Boston lost the county seat, the men of Boston rounded up twenty-four wagons in January of 1874 and raided the city of Elk Falls. They took some furniture and all county records to their town and hid them. One month later the majority of adult men in Boston were arrested and taken back to Elk Falls. The town had no jail so nearly every able-bodied man was deputized to guard over the prisoners in the park. An agreement was eventually reached between the two towns and the records were returned to Elk Falls. For a time the town of Longton, east of Elk Falls and Moline, was also a contender for the county seat.

Between the years of 1870 to nineteen hundred, the residents of Elk and Chautauqua Counties saw Indian nations disappear in land rushes in 1889 and 1893, towns spring up and die when the railroads passed them by and their own version of Carrie Nation, Myra McHenry, go to jail for saloon busting. The town of Grenola was the largest single shipping point for cattle in the United States. Texas drovers were attracted to the town because it cut seventy-five miles off the drive to Emporia. It was a thriving place full of gamblers, drinkers, cattlemen, gunslingers and cowboys until 1885 when the cattle boom moved east to Moline and Longton.

Moline, the southern end of the Atchison, Topeka and Santa Fe line, is just a few miles northeast of Grenola. The town of Moline was mapped out by Major James F. Chapman who determined the layout of the town based on the location of the railroad depot in 1879. Many of the buildings were transferred from the defunct town of Boston, the first structure being a blacksmith shop followed by the post office in May of 1879[2]. That year the first passenger train also pulled into Moline. Like many towns across America, Moline was born and thrived due to the railroad. The frequent trains running through the area allowed fast mail delivery. The old Boston post office which was reestablished in Moline. There were four mail calls a day with train routes running east and west and north and south. The post office was open from 5:30 in the morning until nine at night. Among the stock ranches were the Glenwood, owned by J. C. Jackson northwest of Howard on the Elk River, the Englewood ranch sixteen miles northwest of Howard with 250 acres of prime land owned by Mr. Campbell, the Glen-Elder located fourteen miles northwest of Howard owned by R.F. Glen and the Hillcrest farm two miles north of Howard.[3]

The Town Building was built in 1880 at Main and 2nd street with the top floor used as a social hall and the bottom rented out to various businesses. William Henry Downing and John (George) Hanson had a general merchandise store on the ground floor that also handled grain and livestock called, Downing Hanson Company. In 1885 they took John S. Frazer as a partner in the Moline Store and the trio also established the Moline Bank at that time. Frazer also owned part of the Palace Hotel and considerable real estate in town known as the Frazer Addition in the northwest section of Moline.

John S. Frazer was born on October 24, 1858 in Grape Grove, Ray County, Missouri to William and Sarah Frazer. When he was nineteen in 1877, John went to Ute Creek, Colorado to work cattle with his brother-in-law, Henry Woodruff. His sister, Sarah, and her husband lived in Springer, Colorado (now New Mexico) at that time. The two men worked on a ranch still owned by the Crews (Cabeza de Baca) family located in Bueyeros, New Mexico. In 1879 Frazer drove a herd to New Mexico to sell it and four years later he had the money to buy a herd of his own, which he took back to Ray County, Missouri. With the proceeds from that herd, Frazer moved to Moline, Kansas in the year 1883 right after livestock sale. There appeared to be ample promise in the hilly pastures of Elk County and its railway connections to Kansas City. He was sure of a bright future ahead in Moline and he brought his parents, William and Sarah out to live with him.

Within a short period of time, John Frazer established a good reputation as a businessman. He developed a market for all grades of stock and tried to stimulate feed sales. Frazer and John Colean distributed livestock, corn and coal at the Long Bell Company Old Stand in Moline. When he became partners with William H. Gibson they bought or leased large tracts of land and fenced them off to hold cattle to be brought from Texas. Prior to that time, Frazer had bought local cattle for shipping, but a demand for Texas Longhorns persuaded Gibson and Frazer to take advantage of that market.

While there was some fencing done in Elk and Chautauqua counties, there was also still a large fragment of the free grazing population in the area. The magazine, "The Kansas Farmer", was against using barbed wire and leaned toward open pastures or using orange hedges as border. Fencing off land for imported cattle angered some locals, but on January 28, 1889 Frazer sold his share of The Moline Store to focus entirely on livestock that came from the Texas panhandle.

Frazer had many local partners in the cattle shipping business including the Ames brothers (George and Joseph) and William White and they used area farmers to feed the imported cattle. He felt that he had benefitted the community, but perhaps Frazer was too naive where human resentment was concerned. Social decorum required that people smile and be polite to a person's face, without revealing true sentiments. It was true that he seemed to have a Midas touch with financial matters, as that was Frazer's unique talent. No one wished to murder the artist that painted well or the gunsmith that produced accurate weapons, but dabbling in local economics was a different matter and a risky one.

At any given time, John Frazer had hundreds of thousands of dollars' worth of livestock or real estate and the Howard Bank listed him as one of their major stock holders. While it was true that the Frazers suffered no material wants, they also tried to spread the wealth throughout southeastern Kansas or so they believed. However, many residents of Elk and Chautauqua Counties did not welcome the business of Frazer or his associate, William Gibson, which included importing Texas cattle, fencing and buying up their neighbor's property at sheriff's auctions. There were few economic pies in the area of which John Frazer did not own a slice.

John Frazer was friends with two interesting people in the area, Berndt Olson and Lizzie Bryant. Olson played cards in games organized by John New and people were somewhat spooked by his psychic abilities. Lizzie Bryant dressed like a cowboy and would later win her land near Longton in the 1893 Cherokee Strip land run.

Today, Moline, Howard Sedan are but reflections of the bustling towns they were in the nineteeth century when Frazer and Gibson roamed the area. Moline is located southeast of Wichita, Kansas on highways 99 and 160 with Howard just north on 99 and Sedan south across the county line in Chautauqua County. There are still acres of farm land and open pastures, old one room school houses weathering the passage of time and cemeteries marking towns long gone.

Two

Kansas, the Cattle Industry and Tick Fever

At the heart of the murders of Gibson and Frazer are the cattle industry and a disease known as Texas Fever, Spanish Fever, Splenic Fever, Tick Fever and several other monikers. It was devastating to cattle not exposed to the virus from shortly after birth. Cattle in other states such as Kansas, and even in northern Texas, were susceptible to the disease which was fatal and very contagious in the nineteenth century.

"Between 1850 and 1861, a number of railways were built enabling westernmost towns to interact more with east coast cities. It wasn't until after the Civil War however that these railways became the major routes for people to take. The effects of the improvements in technology and industry related to the railways ultimately led to the first rapid spread of Texas Fever from Texas to Ohio and Texas to New York in just a few weeks. The combination of horse and cattle migration, and the availability of both commercial train and commercial shipping lines turned a once very regional business into a national industry, along with whatever disease patterns accompanied its products. Between 1866 and 1870, this turned Texas Fever in a nationwide epidemic that threatened the entire United States cattle industry, and along with that one of the primary sources of foods for this entire country" [3]

There were several theories about the cause of the illness, such as poor nutrition or poisonous plants eaten by Longhorns while on the trail. Robert Koch of Germany and Louis Pasteur of France had identified bacteria and viruses in the 1880s and developed vaccinations for livestock diseases including chicken cholera and anthrax, so attention was toward scientific solutions. [1] In 1893 Theobald Smith and Fred Lucius Kilborne of the Federal Bureau of Animal Industry in Washington, D.C., isolated the pathogen of Texas fever. They proved that the disease is caused by a microscopic protozoan that inhabits and destroys red blood cells. Smith and Kilborne named the protozoan, *Pyrosoma bigeminum.* It is now recognized that either of two species of the renamed genus *Babesia,* called *Babesia bigemina* and *Babesia bovis,* may be involved in Texas fever. The modern name babesiosis is derived from this, which applies both to Texas Fever and to infections caused throughout the world by these pathogens and other members of the same genus. Besides identifying the microorganism responsible for babesiosis, Smith and Kilborne, discovered that the disease was spread by cattle ticks. After sucking blood from an infected animal, a tick would drop off into the grass and lay eggs from which would hatch young ticks already harboring the protozoan. Weeks after the original tick dropped from its longhorn host, its progeny were still capable of infecting other cattle. Several different species of tick are now known to spread babesiosis. [2]

The symptoms of Texas fever are obvious: high temperatures for four to six days prior to other symptoms, dullness, lack of appetite, decreased milk, pulse fast and weak (ninety to one hundred) and panting. In advanced stages urine turns dark or bloody. Breathe has a fetid odor, accompanied by nervousness and staggering around with cattle refusing to move. Delirium and lethargy follow in later stages. Infected livestock throw their heads around violently, breaking horns and can remain in coma-like position for hours.

The fear and panic caused by the spread of Texas Fever resulted in laws regulating the cattle trails beginning in 1854 and by 1885 Kansas had outlawed cattle drives of Longhorns through Kansas, however, due to the desire to maintain the economic benefits of doing business with Texas ranchers, many amendments to those laws were enacted. The Civil War interrupted further refinement of those laws and the demand for cattle in the eastern states spurred a need to reconcile the desire to do business, and at the same time, protect Kansas livestock. As Skaggs notes,

"1866 led to revision of Kansas law that allowed entrance to all cattle breeds to take advantage of the railroads being used to transport cattle to pens in Abilene, Ellsworth, Dodge City, Kansas City and Wichita. The mass trailing through the state led again to outbreaks of Tick Fever." [4]

In January 1885 Kansas Representative W.D. Platt introduced House Bill 116,

"An act for the protection of cattle against Texas, Splenic or Spanish Fever." The law stipulated that between March 1 and December 1 that any persons driving cattle through Kansas capable of spreading Texas Fever would be guilty of a fine of between $100 and $2000 and/or imprisonment from thirty days to one year. Provisions to recover civil damages was covered under the act." [4]

So on the one hand there were armed ranchers guarding the established trails to ensure that cattle did not stray from the legal boundaries, but also those such as, Joseph McCoy, of the Abilene stockyards ensuring that the dreaded Texas cattle made it north. The result was that there were more outbreaks of Tick Fever with $63,000,000 cattle lost to Texas Fever between 1866 and 1889.

> "Desperate cattlemen drove cattle clear up to Wyoming. Losses due to Texas Fever took a toll up north in Wyoming as well which had no quarantine laws. Kansas ranchers informed Texas cattlemen they could take their cattle elsewhere.

In 1867 Kansas amended the 1866 law which had opened access to Texas herds placed a quarantine line through Kansas along the sixth principal meridian or 97°22' allowing south Texas cattle to be driven to Ellsworth, Wellington and Wichita. New lines were drawn as population shifted westward. The desire to protect Kansas herds conflicted with the desire to keep income from Texas ranchers.

> "Despite efforts to restrict movement of Texas Longhorns more than half of Kansas was still open to diseased cattle. Laws were not strictly enforced and many were in denial due to a need to retain money from the Texas cattle industry." [4]

With the high risk of importing southern Texas cattle and the hostility of local ranchers toward the Longhorn breed it does not seem like a good business decision to continue to import them, but profit was a strong motivator. The herds in the eastern states had been decimated by the Civil War and demand for Midwestern beef was still high by the time Kansas banned cattle drives through the state in 1885. The railroads offered a safe alternative method of transporting Longhorns through the state with limited contact with local breeds. According to Thomas Etheredge of Restoration Farms in Sedgwick County Kansas, Frazer could pick up Longhorns in Texas for $30 to $40 a head and sell them to meatpacking plants in Chicago for $300 to $400 a head. It would be hard to realize that sort of profit from any other venture at the time.

Tick Fever was one motivator behind the murders of William Gibson and John Frazer. A second issue was the fencing off of property they did to contain their cattle in an area where free grazing was still favored among cattlemen. Cattle that were grass fed and roamed free were generally healthier than those contained and fed commercial grain.

The third motivator was the efforts of Wesley Best to introduce the Hereford cattle breed to Kansas, particularly Elk and Chautauqua Counties. Best had bought two bulls from Herefordshire, England in 1882 and three females to produce a line of thoroughbred Herefords. While it was true that Herefords nicked (bred) well with Longhorns, it was no longer necessary for cattle to be trail tough. He had stopped mixing the two breeds when orders for the thoroughbreds began coming in. Best had only been raising Herefords for a year before Frazer moved to Elk County.

The railroads put an end to the need for Texas longhorns as far as Best was concerned. Cattle that rode to market did not require endurance. The meat of the British cattle tasted better and Herefords thrived on forage, which also meant that Frazer's feed was not necessary. Of course, if Frazer and Gibson had their way only a few would own enough land for grazing. Everyone else would need to purchase feed, especially during droughts and bad winters. Herefords also matured early and so they were ready for market and breeding earlier as well. Best had first seen the breed in 1876 at the Centennial Exposition in Philadelphia and believed they were the future of cattle ranching.

Frazer and Gibson had doubts that Tick Fever was the illness that infected local cattle. While it could turn the urine red from hemolysis, it did not cause hemorrhaging from orifices on the animal s body. Anthrax and Texas Fever were similar illnesses with many of the same symptoms until the last stages of the diseases. Frazer did not trust Wesley Best. While the man was a good rancher, he was more of a risk taker than Frazer who chose to buy low and sell high. The cattle Best bought from Britain were costly and though they would eventually turn a good profit and breed well with Longhorns, Herefords were still new to the United States. Best planned to dominate the market with Herefords, preferably his Herefords. But Frazer wasn't frightened off. The Longhorn market was well established and he had many good customers who still wanted his livestock.

The newspaper article of June 27, 1890 in the *Moline Republican* [6] had not been read by most people until that evening, but it would fan the flames in the uproar over Texas Fever. That day Frazer had managed to miss both Keenan Hurst, the State Veterinarian Surgeon (from the Livestock Sanitary Commission) and the President of the Livestock Sanitary Board in his trek around the county to survey damage from the fever. Their findings supported the claims of Best and other ranchers that it was indeed Tick Fever. Wesley Best was a friend of Hurst, the Livestock Commissioner, so Frazer's concerns were not without foundation. There was some confusion over whether the cattle in Elk County were from Texas, it seems only the Ames cattle were imported from southern Texas. All other herds were from New Mexico, which did not carry the fever. (The Moline Republican (Moline, Kansas) July 4, 1890)[7]

William Harrison Gibson was born September 6, 1840 in Pope County, Illinois. He was a Civil War veteran having served in Company M, 13th Illinois Volunteer Cavalry. G.A.R. Post #461 (1891-1916) in Leeds, Kansas was named in his honor. He was mustered out as a 2nd Lieutenant in Pilot Knob, Missouri on August 31, 1865. He married Harriet Jackson with whom he had eleven children, nine which survived him. Gibson would be known as the wealthiest man in Elk County being involved in banking, real estate and livestock. At the time of his death Gibson was worth $30,000 according to the probate papers filed in Chautauqua County on March 31, 1911.

It took some time to settle the estates of both Gibson and Frazer with outstanding debts, such as $4000 due to the Central Loan and Debenture Company of Kansas City as owed by Gibson.

The ongoing legal fees and payments to expert witnesses also depleted their estates. The law firm of John Downing McBrian handled the Gibson estate, which was held at auction on October 7, 1890 by George D. Hoy. McBrian would also serve as the chaplain at Lansing for eight years where he was much respected.

Three

The Murder of William Harrison Gibson

On Friday May 30, 1890 the *Howard Courant* ran the headline, "W.H. Gibson Dead-Sudden and Unexpected Death of One of Our Oldest Citizens."[1] The sub headline stated he was found dead in his Central hotel room the previous Friday, which was May 23, 1890.

Gibson had arrived in Moline on Thursday night, May 22 with his daughter, Mahala, on the train from Eureka, a town northwest from Moline. He had been in Eureka for two days with Walter S. Lambert, a loan officer from Moline. They were establishing the new Farmers' and Drover's Bank at Eureka with the shareholders where Gibson would be the head cashier. Lambert had dined with Gibson in Eureka and rode the train with him, but got off in Howard. Lambert received a telegram informing him of Gibson's death from George Martin, who also summoned the coroner as he would be a witness in the case. Martin was a cashier at the Moline Bank.

When Gibson checked into the Central Hotel with his daughter, Mahala, Thursday night he was given a room across the street from the hotel office by the porter, Eddy Harris, who escorted Gibson there between nine and ten o'clock after a large supper. According to Harris, Gibson was in good spirits, laughing and joking with friends and healthy. His room had two beds with one unoccupied. He planned to rise early for the trip home before breakfast, which was ten miles southeast of Moline. He left instruction for the liveryman, Charles L. Lane, to deliver his team to the hotel, but then Gibson had not appeared. Lane was a partner of Wesley Best in selling Herefords and later became a veterinarian in Coffeyville, Kansas in 1900. When he still had not appeared by 7:20 am, Mahala, who was very concerned as her father usually was never late, and the landlady, Anna Pancake, knocked on the door with no response.

The hotel manager, Solon Francis Thompson, was told of the circumstances and he broke into the room. Gibson was found deceased on his bed wearing only underwear with no signs of violence or foul play. His clothes were neatly folded and placed under his pillow.

Thompson had been a colonel in the Confederate army serving with General Morgan's band. He was captured by the Union army and held captive in Chicago where he managed to bribe a guard and escape. When he later returned for his comrades, the helpful guard had been executed as a traitor and Thompson was apprehended once again to be placed in a dungeon. Unwilling to accept this fate, he and some other prisoners tunneled out and returned to Kentucky to find that Morgan's band was broken up, so Thompson formed his own. In a skirmish with Yankees, a union soldier was killed. Thompson was nearly executed, but was saved by his wife's appeals to the governor.

The coroner, Dr. Franklin S. Olney was summoned from Howard and arrived by 11 a.m. and was assisted by Dr. William

H. Smethers of Moline during the postmortem examination. The initial exam provided no clue as to the sudden demise of Gibson, except for an enlarged spleen and some corrosion of the stomach lining, which Olney attributed to postmortem gastric juices. Olney had let the stomach lay unattended for days with the intention of having chemical analysis done, but finally threw the organ out minus the lab tests. It thus appeared Gibson died of heart failure despite no previous symptoms or health complaints. [2]

On May 23, 1890 the coroner's jury determined the cause of death as unknown. The coroner's jury consisted of Albert B. Good, Edward M. Shearer, W.H. Potter, A. F. McClaslin, Charles Aker, Dr. H.N. Mason. The body was released to his family where the funeral was held at the Gibson home. The funeral was conducted by the Masonic and Odd Fellows orders.

William Harrison Gibson was born on September 6, 1840 in Polk County, Illinois and came to Howard County, Kansas in April 1871. Engaging in farming, stock and eventually the loan business, Gibson was the wealthiest man in Chautauqua County. He was survived by his wife, Harriet and nine of eleven children. Evidence of Gibson's active career as a banker can be seen in the May 28, 1890 edition of the *Sedan Graphic* [3] on page three in advertisements for real estate loans. It is one of many such advertisements.

It is interesting to note that Dr. Olney had been accused of poisoning a man's coffee with rat poison in July 1888, since it would later be suggested that Gibson drank poisoned lemonade. An empty glass of it had been found in the hotel room, which Anna Pancake stated she brought to Gibson. Dr. Olney also owned his own pharmacy, further causing doubt about natural causes.

Dr. Olney was accused of poisoning U.A. Buckingham, a local painter, in February 1888 along with this wife, Etta, Ervin H. Dickson and George Walters (Etta's father-in-law). Dickson confessed the last week of February 1890 prompting the arrest and preliminary hearing of the suspects March 5th and 6th in Judge Baker's court. Buckingham it seems failed to support his family and his wife had filed for divorce. After several plans to murder him that included using a pistol, it was decided to eliminate Buckingham with poison and it was at that point Olney became involved. The first attempts failed as Dickson did not use both packs of powder provided by Olney to place in his whisky. Buckingham suffered from pain and seizures, but pulled through. Additional attempts using large amounts of chloroform seemed to be inadequate as well, but a few weeks later Buckingham finally died.

The courts eventually determined that Buckingham died from uremia, a kidney disease of which the deceased suffered similar symptoms, such as severe back pain. Dr. Smethers was one of the physicians testifying against the notion Buckingham was murdered. Since the reputation of Dickson (also spelled Dixon) for truth telling was poor, the case was eventually dismissed in October 1890 by the County Attorney Reuben Harrison Nicholson and Judge Troup. The entire case was based on the confession of Ervin Dickson.

The death investigation of William H. Gibson was not as extensive as the later murder of John S. Frazer and may never have had the legendary status propelling the story into the future if it had not been for the brutality and clear homicide of Frazer's demise. Conspiracies were already looming with such groups as the *Livestock Protective Association* being behind the murders, which was formed shortly before the two cattlemen imported Texas cattle into Kansas in February 1890.[4]

William Harrison Gibson May 22, 1890 at the Central
Hotel, Moline, KS. Partner of John Samuel Frazer.
Provided by Gibson family.

Hiram Sparks McCray Born: November 30, 1849 in Hancock County, Indiana. Died: 1931 in Fredonia, Wilson County, Kansas. Sheriff of Wilson County. New told his story about the murders to him when arrested in 1896. (Find a Grave)

Dr. Milton Trowbridge Evans Born: February 1859 in Illinois. Died: April 23, 1934. Did inquest of Frazer in 1890. Testified at 1896 hearing. (Find a Grave)

John Downing McBrian Born: September 10, 1840 in Mount Vernon, Illinois. Died: March 20, 1921 in Sedan, Kansas. Attorney for Gibson estate. Also a minister. Chaplain at Lansing for eight years. A freemason as many in the area. McBrian was also assistant district attorney for Chautauqua County. (Find a Grave)

Daniel M. Woodworth Born: April 15, 1845 Died: February 16, 1932 in Sedan, Kansas. His surname was originally, Glasgow. Changed it after running away from home in 1859. Post commander of Stones River, Kansas GAR 1923. Witness at 1896 trial.
(Find a Grave)

Willis Edmund (Bud) Baker Born September 30, 1872 in Carrollton, Carroll, Missouri. March 27, 1961 in Pawhuska, Osage, Oklahoma. He was with Brown June 18, 1890 when they saw Burgess. (Find a Grave)

Enos Bell Munday Born: September 18, 1854 in Glascow, Illinois. Died: October 8, 1932 in Cedarvale, Kansas Witness in 1890 for Frazer being missing. Saw Frazer that morning. He was also an acquaintance of Frazer's.
(Find a Grave)

Wesley Best Ranch Handbook of Southeastern Kansas
(Kansas State Historical Society)

John Francis Colean Born: 1855 in Madison County, Illinois. Died: 1891 in Burden, Kansas. Buried in Girard, KS. In business with Frazer in the Moline Feed store. Wife granted a divorce in 1891 with custody of children. Death under mysterious circumstances. (Kansas State Historical Society)

Rev. William Clark Goodwin Born: September 3, 1837 in New York. Died: May 12, 1913 in Moline, Kansas. Minister at Methodist Episcopal Church in Moline. Wrote memorial to Frazer. Served in the 92nd Regiment in New York. (Find a Grave)

Silas Edward Walker Born: October 26, 1856 in Illinois. Died: October 31, 1931 in Vinita, Oklahoma. Lived in Sedan and was a blacksmith. (Find a Grave) Walker discovered the coat and vest of John Frazer 250 yards from pool where body was found. Was with Frank Hendricks. (Find a Grave)

Thomas Jefferson Hudson Born: October 13, 1839 in Jamestown, Indiana. Died: January 4, 1923 in Wichita, Kansas. Defense council in 1896 trial. (Find a Grave)

Samuel Walter Leake Born: September 5, 1864 in Richmond, Ray County, Missouri. Died: April 7, 1929 in Dixonville, Oregon. Worked for Frazer and saw him that Friday morning. Described his clothing at inquest and habit of carrying a check book and gold watch. He was Frazer's nephew. Moved to Oregon in 1890. (Find a Grave)

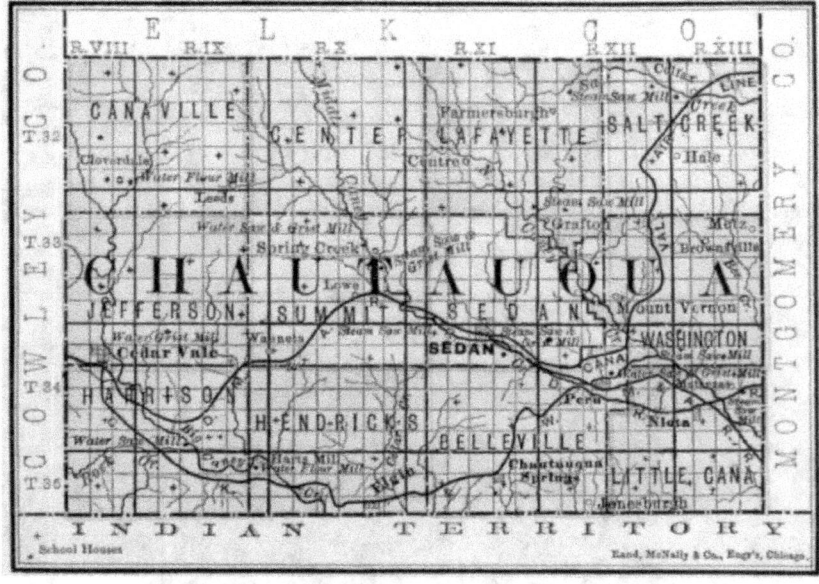

Chautauqua County Kansas (Kansas State Historical Society)

Lewis Hanback Born: March 27, 1839 in Scott County, Illinois. Died: September 7, 1897 in Topeka, Kansas Sent by Governor Humphrey to investigate Frazer murder in response to rumors of political motivations. (Find a Grave)

Charles Harvey Sherwin Testified at inquest that he saw blood on John Grissom's shirt sleeve in Sedan, Kansas.
(Find a Grave)

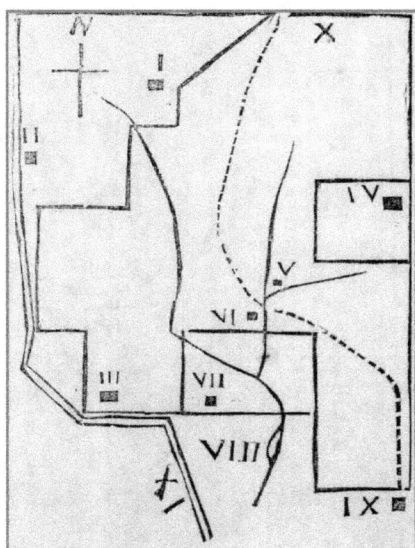

Frazer Crime Scene Map I. Binn's Cabin II. Goodell's Farm III. Patch of weeks where Frazer's body was hidden IV. Spring V. Hammond's Farm VI. Pool in Deer Creek where body was found. VII. J. Burgess house VIII. Gate into pasture where Frazer entered IX. Moline-Sedan Road (now 99 highway) X Residence of W.A. Gray Dotted line is Old Trail through Hunter's Canyon Map on next page from the Moline Republican
(The Moline Republican Friday, July 4, 1890)

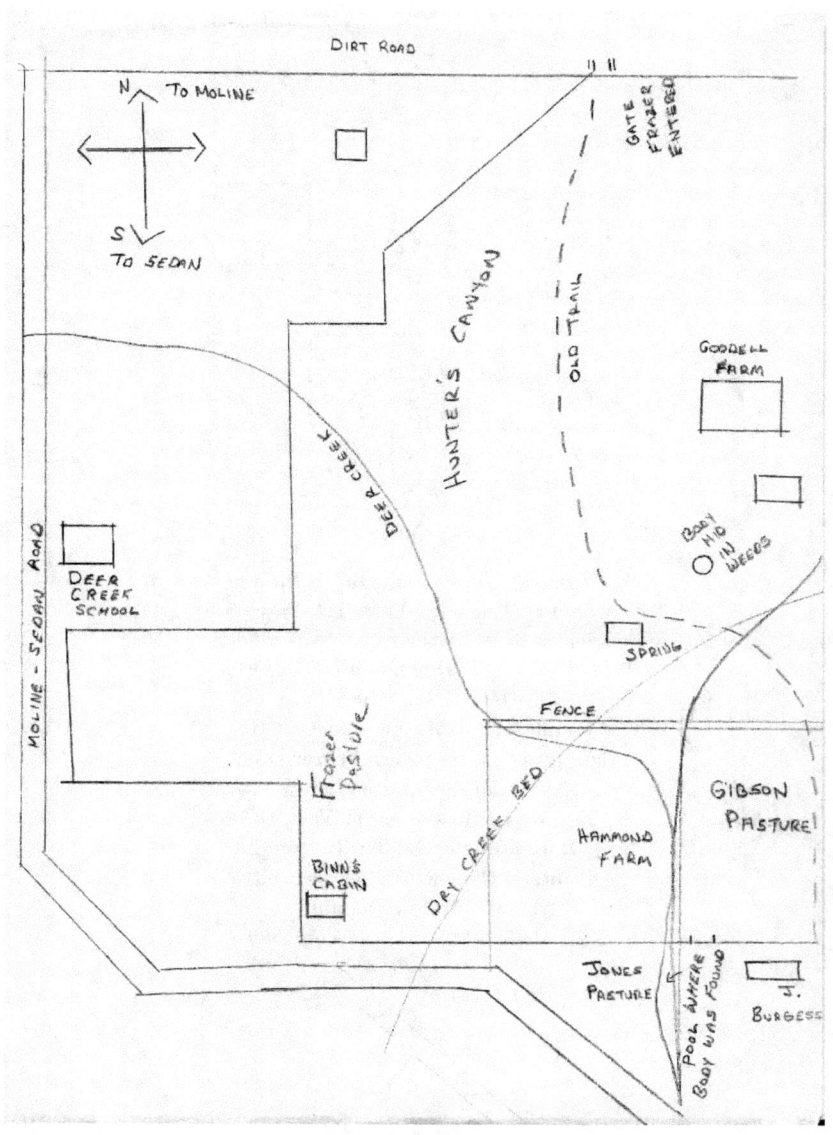

Author map showing more details of crime scene.

Reuben Harrison Nicholson, Elk County Prosecutor and later defense attorney.

Peter Ellis McGrew (Ellis) Lived in Summit, Center Township, Chautauqua County in 1880. Testified that he owned a knife that was lost near the pool in Deer Creek.

Four

The Murder and Inquest of John Samuel Frazer

The front page headline of the *Weekly Times Star* (Sedan) on July 4, 1890[1] announced in bold print that John S. Frazer had been waylaid by cowards and assassinated by being stabbed to death. The board of Chautauqua County Commissioners offered a $1000 reward for capture of the killer or killers and made it clear that the homicide of such a respected man would not go unpunished.

William Jones found the corpse as he was riding fence for repairs on June 30, 1890. It was found floating face down in a waist high pool of water in Deer Creek in an area known as Hunter's Canyon a mile and a half northwest of Sedan. It was off an eighty-five acre pasture on the Neal Roe (Row) farm between the Roe house and a house owned by the Arch Hammond (Hamon) family. The area was full of timber and thick underbrush and high weeds. Jones "gave the alarm", which alerted search parties in the area and soon after a large crowd gathered at the scene.

Thomas N. King, the Justice of the Peace in Sedan in Chautauqua County, assembled a jury for an inquest. The body lay midstream, covered in a pool of water, around thirty inches deep, in a bent over position, except for the back of the head and neck. After floating the body over to the creek bank, a blanket was slipped under it for examination. When Frazer first went missing it was assumed that he had succumbed to the intense summer heat and lay dead or sick in a pasture somewhere, but once the corpse was rolled over the knife wounds made it apparent that the death was not natural. According to the *Cedar Vale Commercial,* Frazer had been stabbed eleven times. Once in the abdomen, twice near the lower sternum and eight times in the cardiac area with his throat slit from ear to ear. [4]. The heart was penetrated and it appeared someone had taken the knife and moved it back and forth to cut the organ open. Curiously, *Cedar Vale Commercial* mentioned that it was thus impossible for Frazer to have committed suicide. [4] The body was fully dressed except for his hat, coat and vest, which Frazer was known to wear. The hat was found with blood on the rim near the bank on a gravel bed, but the light colored vest and coat were nowhere to be seen. The hat also bore a bloody hand print. The article in the Cedar Vale newspaper mentioned something not found in other sources; that Frazer's pocket knife was discovered in his pants pocket with blood on it, possibly prompting the reference to suicide. [5] The pool in Deer Creek was a popular swimming hole and a make shift diving board remained there. Though the area was remote, those familiar with the creek would have known of the pool despite the brush concealing it.

The onsite observation by the coroner's jury of the crime scene was procedure at the time for investigating a murder. When no further evidence was discovered at the scene the body was removed to the courthouse for further examination by the coroner and for official identification. A dense crowd was present at the courthouse inquest. Witnesses who were interviewed identified the body as that of John S. Frazer.

To construct a timeline of events, King interviewed witnesses in which the first was Joe Debenbrink who lived in Wauneta and was a long time business associate of Frazer's. He also was among those who identified the body. Debenbrink stated that he had received a letter from Frazer Thursday, June 26 stating that he needed to get the cattle he was feeding ready to ship. On Friday afternoon Frazer sent a young man named Henry Means with a message for Debenbrink expect to see him on Saturday. [2]

Another sworn witness was Enos Bell Munday, who was also an acquaintance of Frazer's. He had last seen the man on Saturday, June 28th between the hours of six and seven in the morning at his residence one half mile east of the Gibson place going south on the Moline-Sedan road (now highway 99). Frazer had asked Munday to go and assist the Gibson boys in hauling hay that morning. Munday reported Frazer's mood and health as good.

John W. Glenn, who also lived on the Moline-Sedan road some two and a fourth miles from the Gibson farm, stated he saw Frazer on horseback heading toward Sedan around eight in the morning. They only exchanged greetings. Glenn was an acquaintance of Frazer's.

Frazer's brother, William F. Frazer was also questioned. He stated that he saw his brother on Friday, June 27 when they travelled to Howard together. That afternoon John told his brother he was "going south", meaning to Sedan in Chautauqua County, through his large land holdings of some 8000 acres where he kept cattle. William recalled that John had $20.00 with him and a gold watch. He was single and thirty-two years old. Their parents lived around two and half miles north of Moline. John was wearing a light colored jacket and hat when William saw him last. He too identified the body as that of his brother, John Frazer.[3]

An employee of Frazer's, Samuel Walter Leake, saw Frazer that Friday morning wearing the same clothing as described by the other witnesses and also added that he usually wore a gold watch and carried a checkbook as well as a memorandum book with him. It is interesting to note that the newspapers did not mention that Leake was Frazer's nephew from his half-sister, Isabelle from Ray County, Missouri. Right after the murder he left for Roseburg, Oregon to live with family there (Bellis and Parrott) where he farmed.

The man who found the body between nine and ten o'clock, William Riley Jones, was mending fences when he located Frazer's corpse. Jones lived on the Roe place near Sedan. He stated he could only see the head and shoulders of the body and he was not familiar with Frazer.

Justice King cleared the courtroom of spectators so that a team of doctors, Caleb Sipple, John Sharpless and John Graham, could further complete the autopsy. The post mortem examination determined that the knife wounds penetrated the chest cavity several times with one wound directly through the heart, several thrusts through the intestines, and the throat slit so deep the windpipe was nearly severed. Before allowing the doctors to announce their decision on cause of death, King stated that further testimony would be delayed and the jury reconvened at a later time for further investigation.

On Tuesday, June 24, 1890, Frazer had stepped off the train in Moline after shipping cattle to Kansas City. He immediately heard the talk of huge losses in cattle from Texas Fever in Chautauqua County spread by his herd.[7] Instead of going home after the long trip, Frazer rode south to check out the situation and did not return home until 2 am Thursday morning, appearing worn and haggard. He spent that Thursday morning in Howard and elsewhere arranging funds to repay the losses. When seeing the dead cattle at the Best ranch he cried, "Mr. Best, I will pay you and all the others for all the losses that may be caused by fever from my cattle." He made the same promise to the men in Moline. He spent Thursday night his parent's house in Moline where his mother Sarah stated that she was worried about his safety. The following conversation ensued according to the *Moline Republican,*

> John Frazer: Mother, I supposed it will break me up, but I must make those men good. If it takes every cent."

Sarah Frazer: Act honorably, if it takes all.

> John: Don't worry mother, I can take care of you and father if I have nothing left. (William Frazer was age 82).

Sarah: John, do you think you are safe down there?"

John: None too safe, but I must go."

When Frazer left Friday morning he told his parents he would return in two to four days. The first stop was the Best ranch and then the other farmers with losses. While at the Best ranch Frazer asked what promises Mr. Gibson had made to which Best replied Gibson had stated he would pay for every head that died [8]. He spent Friday night at Harriet Gibson's place where he told, William Latelle, a Gibson employee, "It looks like they got away with Mr. Gibson-don't you think they will kill me? I am not afraid." During the night Frazer heard the dogs barking strangely and fearing an intruder was outside went for a shotgun, but it had no ammunition. That Saturday morning he rose and began his trek to reimburse his neighbors and check on his herd, which turned out to be a fatal errand.

The only known fact at that time was that John S. Frazer was in business with William H, Gibson, who had been allegedly murdered months earlier in Moline. Because the two men had been involved in transporting Texas Longhorns that carried Texas fever, most people assumed the two cases were related. The two had received numerous death threats through letters and talk of how the two men needed to be killed had been heard in the area. There did not seem to be any other reason anyone would want to murder Frazer, particularly in such a brutal manner.

Five

The Investigation Begins in Chautauqua County 1890

On Friday night, June 27, 1890, John Frazer spent the night with the family of his former partner, William Gibson, on their farm between Moline and Sedan. He left early as testimony indicated with him being first seen around six in the morning by Enos Munday heading toward the Gibson land north of Sedan. It was surmised that Frazer probably entered the pasture just after eight o'clock to check on his cattle. This was routine behavior and no one was concerned until Frazer's mare was found Sunday afternoon roaming the field still wearing a saddle and bridle by James Burgess who was the caretaker of the Gibson property. Sheriff Lowe initiated a search as it was feared Frazer had succumbed to the stifling heat and was lying either sick or dead somewhere. A larger search party of forty or fifty men, including some from Moline, was organized

Monday morning and began combing the area, but Jones accidently found the body first while mending fences. He had not assumed that Frazer was a murder victim.

That Saturday afternoon before the body was discovered, Miss Lena Goodell, who lived with her father, was outside when she heard two strange wails between 9 am and 10 am, Saturday June 28 coming from the canyon. Her father, John Woodworth Goodell was on Frazer's coroner's jury and a Civil War veteran having served in Company G of the 91st Regiment Illinois Volunteer Infantry as a 1st Lieutenant. Lena called for him after hearing the screams, but Goodell did not hear anything even after running in the direction of the ravine west of their house. At the bottom of the ravine (known as Hunter's Canyon) was a creek. The area was remote and difficult to access and when her father heard no further sounds he dismissed the matter. Kansas is known for being "flat", however, the hills in Chautauqua County are steeper than they appear and rocky.

The theory was that Frazer was murdered in the pasture that afternoon, then the body moved that night and tossed in the creek. His black horse was found with the halter strap gone, apparently cut off near the north gate. His checkbook was in a saddle pocket and his raincoat strapped to the saddle.

On July 1, 1890, the County Commissioners offered a reward of $1000[2] for the arrest and conviction of the murder or murderers of John S. Frazer. The next day the sheriff arrested John and Thomas Grissom and Wilson A. Gray on a warrant for the murder. Grounds for the arrest were unknown aside from the fact that all three lived near the crime scene.

On Wednesday afternoon, July 2, 1890 around forty men from the Elk County and Moline area gathered in Sedan after searching the region north of Sedan for clues regarding the Frazer murder. The one suspect the posse tracked turned out to already be in the

Chautauqua County jail, Wilson Gray. In the crowd that day in Sedan were the two brothers of the deceased, William and Thomas Frazer, Sheriff Oley Richolson, Senator Roe and Attorney Dan Carr. There was no shortage of outrage about the murder of Frazer with citizens of two counties demanding justice for him, in spite of the fury over Tick Fever. The reward of $1000 more than likely prompted a great deal of the enthusiasm. [1]

The Preliminary Hearings

The preliminary hearing for Wilson Gray was on Saturday July 5, 1890 which resulted in a dismissal due to lack of evidence [3]. A witness for the prosecution, Mrs. John Greer, testified that Gray passed her place that Saturday morning on the day of the murder between nine and ten o'clock going west toward Spring Creek. The state had made quite an issue of Gray's feelings about importing Texas cattle, so someone placing him near the scene at that time was crucial.

In his defense, Gray testified that he had plowed a patch of cane until seven-thirty that morning then he went to the Spring Creek post office arriving there an hour later. He presented a number of witnesses who saw him at eight-thirty that morning and others who stated he had been in town until four o'clock in the afternoon. Gray could not have committed the murder.

The hearing for the Grissom brothers was Monday July 7, 1890. One of the deputies present at the arrest of the Grissoms was Ben Adams who testified that John Grissom stated that he and his brother were fishing on the North Caney Friday and camped all night. [4] They arrived home around eight o'clock Saturday morning. John was accompanied by his brother Tom, their father and a younger brother. A man named Captain John Greer who (husband of the earlier witness and whose land the Gibson-Frazer were fed March 1890) lived six miles northwest from Sedan near the Grissoms stated that he did not see them that Friday night, but they were at his house that Saturday evening until ten o'clock that night.

The state presented a witness, Charles Sherwin, who saw John Grissom in Sedan in front of E. C. Ackerman's implement store with a stain on the left sleeve of his shirt two inches long and half an inch wide. It looked like a blood stain. Sherwin called the attention of Sam Conners and Oran Sumner to it and later told a man named, Alonzo Kilmer. Another witness, W.H. Aiken, also stated that he saw John Grissom there on July 1st, 1890. Grissom told him that he had started walking through a pasture and brush, but the heat got to him and he turned back. He also stated that he knew who two of the killers were. Aiken said Grissom spoke of being at a neighbor's house the Saturday before the murder where the woman stated that Gibson was dead and Frazer would not live long. At that time, Keenen Hurst came up to Grissom and stated that some men from Moline were looking for him and his brother. John stated that he would return home and then "go see those fellows".

Harry Turner testified that he heard John Grissom talking to Mr. McGreer. [5] He said that he could take authorities to people who knew something about the killers if they would go. Turner saw the stain on Grissom's shirt sleeve. After William Jones testified about finding the body, Alonzo Kilmer took the stand stating that he knew the defendants. He saw Thomas Grissom in Sedan Tuesday after the murder with his father. Grissom wanted to sell his crop and move away. Kilmer also saw what appeared to be a blood stain on Grissom's shirt. Another state witness, William R. Hillman, testified that he was at Ackerman's on Saturday, but did not see the Grissom brothers then. He saw them Tuesday after the murder. The father and brothers were in the store buying cartridges for a revolver because John told Hillman that he had come very close to being in that pasture the day Frazer was killed. The father wanted to trade the revolver for a Winchester. (Moline Republican, July 11, 1890)

The defense countered with their own witnesses to persuade the jury that the Grissom family had no part in the homicide. The head of the family, Solomon Grissom, stated that he was a farmer living seven miles north of Sedan and northwest of the pasture where Frazer was murdered. He was not a cattle owner and not a member of the Alliance. He had been fishing and camping with his sons on the North Caney that Friday night where they arrived around ten o'clock. They camped near the home of Van Haines where they caught a few fish. Grissom was on the river with Tom, John and one of his younger boys. He then took his sons home.

Saturday morning Solomon saw Haines around seven o'clock and then Grissom went directly home. On the way he passed the house of Mr. Paton and Clark Walker going west then angled off to the southwest and then turned south. Grissom entered his property through the east gate around nine o'clock Saturday morning. He never went any nearer to the crime scene pasture than his house and never saw Frazer on the way home. Frazer would have entered on the west side. At around ten o'clock a man named Roscoe Greer returned a corn planter and weeding hoe. His sons John and Tom were home all day Saturday. He then went to John Greer's house at seven that night and stayed until eleven o'clock. When asked about why he said that his sons knew more than they were saying, Grissom was referring to the fence cutting and not the murder. The men had considered standing guard, but decided not to do so.

Taking the stand next was Mrs. Emily Grissom, wife of Solomon Grissom. She testified that her son, John, had on the same clothes that Tuesday before he was arrested. He had only one change of clothes, which she brought to him the Saturday before. After hearing talk about the stained shirt she advised him not to change until after the trial. She was positive he was wearing the same outfit. Her sons did not know they were under arrest when the sheriff took them from home Wednesday morning.

When John Grissom took the stand he stated that he was 23 years old and had lived in the area some time. He had been at home with his parents since February 13, 1890. That Friday, June 27, he was in Sedan then went fishing on the North Caney around two o'clock that afternoon. He camped that night on the river. The next Saturday morning he saw Haines and his wife and he had also seen Haines the night before. That morning they also saw John Lorie and then passed by Walker's house where they had seen some women standing in the doorway. He repeated his father's description of their way home arriving around nine o'clock. John did nothing until the afternoon when he pulled weeds. Grissom stated that he had on the same clothes, except for a vest he had been wearing and he had no idea of what the stain on his shirt wrist band was from. He was at no time anywhere near the Gibson pasture where Frazer was killed that Saturday. Roscoe Greer had come over and asked him to go Sedan and they men attempted the walk, but after about fifteen yards the heat was too intense and they turned back. John stated that he had been to town the night before and did not care to return at that time. If they had gone to town the men would have had to travel through the Gibson pasture around the time of the murder. Monday morning Grissom met Enos Munday on the road who told him not to go search unless he had been deputized [6].

Van Haines testified that he saw John and Tom Grissom a week ago on the North Caney on Friday afternoon and Saturday morning. Haines had some sick cattle requiring him to stay up late and rise early the next morning. When out inspecting the cattle Haines saw the brothers still sleeping on the riverbank. He returned home for breakfast and then saw the Grissom's later and talked with them.

John Lorie stated that he lived a quarter of a mile from Haines. He knew the Grissoms and saw them in Haine's yard last Saturday, but was not sure of the time since he had no time piece. Testifying next was Robert Payton who lived six miles north of Sedan, three quarters of a mile from the Grissom place and two miles north of the Gibson pasture. He was familiar with the Grissoms and their team and saw them last Saturday around eight in the morning. The Payton house stood some twenty yards from the road from where Robert saw "The two boys and old gent pass by in the wagon." He also was not sure of the time.

Roscoe Greer verified the Grissom story about him returning the planter and hoe around nine last Saturday morning. Greer saw the entire family there then returned home at noon. The defense rested and Justice King dismissed the charges due to lack of evidence.

Motives

Early on motivations for the murders of Gibson and Frazer were the dozens of dead Kansas cattle that had come into contact with Texas Longhorns. In the forefront was Wesley Best who lost some forty head after feeding in the same pastures as the Frazer Longhorns. On March 17 the Frazer cattle were placed in the field owned by Best and fed there until mid-April, then around June 1st after the Texas cattle were gone, Best, placed his own cattle in the field for pasture. After two weeks those cattle became sick and died. The hay and residue left over from the Frazer cattle had been saturated with ticks, which soon infested the local cattle. George Satterlee was another rancher with the same issue and there were many others. The problem appeared to be with local cattle being placed in the same fields where the Texas cattle had been fed the prior spring and winter. Native cattle in contact with the Longhorns that summer were not affected.

By July 11, 1890 the missing coat and vest had still not been found. Those seeking to solve the mystery or collect the reward believed they had found the location of the murder and where the perpetrators had hid until Frazer approached. They also surmised that the killers had waited in the brush until night fall to move the body to the pool where it was found in the ravine. The area of the ambush was probably where Frazer would have gone to cross the creek. There was also a spring nearby.

The three men previously arrested for the crime had been set free after being interrogated. Gray was interviewed on Thursday, July 3 before Justice King with the district attorney, McBrian, bringing forth a multitude of witnesses, but no evidence to connect Gray with the murder. The examination ran from Thursday evening until that Saturday at 9 am when it reconvened.

Gray took the stand on the advice of his lawyer, John V. Beckman, another Civil War veteran having served in the 47th Illinois from 1861 to 1864, and described in minute detail where he had been on June 28th from 5 a.m. until after dark. Beckman presented witnesses to collaborate his alibi and Justice King released Gray. On Monday July 7, the prosecution questioned the Grissom brothers, John and Thomas in much the same manner with the same results. Roscoe Greer testified that he saw a man on horseback around 9 am on Old Trail (In Hunter's Canyon). Was at the Grissom place 9 am to noon that Saturday returning a hoe and planter.

The witnesses only added the information that around the time of the murder four men were seen at a deserted house north of the Gibson pasture. Also noticed was a trail leading south through the Hammond pasture, just south of Frazer's land made by four men on horseback. There was a second trail that ran parallel to it about three feet apart with blood on the grass between them. There was no real evidence to link them to the crime and the Grissom brothers were released.

Also on that Monday the coroner's jury convened on June 28th was recalled with the final decision being that John S. Frazer was indeed murdered by persons unknown. The jury stated that,

"John S. Frazer came to his death in Chautauqua County, Kansas on June 1890 by being feloniously stabbed and cut by some sharp instrument by the hand of some party or parties unknown". *[Weekly Times Star, July 11, 1890]*

The members of the coroner's jury were, Eli C. Ackerman (Foreman), John W. Taylor, James B. Cannon, J.Q. Adams, John W. Goodell and John R. Cowell with King as acting coroner.

The general consensus at time was that there was a conspiracy to murder Frazer and eventually the criminals would either confess due to guilt or simply talk too much to the wrong people. The notion of a conspiracy still remains the opinion of many whose ancestors lived in Elk and Chautauqua Counties. February 28, 1890, after Gibson and Frazer brought a herd of Texas cattle to the area, the local Farmer's Alliance held a meeting where angry members passed strong resolutions determining the people to be the law. This action, of course, led many to anticipate trouble. The deadline for importing Texas cattle was March 1, so technically Gibson and Frazer did nothing illegal, however, the mild winter made local farmers extremely concerned for the health of their cattle. The Alliance requested that the two men not bring Texas cattle to the area, but were ignored.

The cattle from Texas were not immediately landed in Kansas as seems to be the assumption, but in the Indian Territory south of Coffeyville at Lenepaugh. After that the cattle were taken to Arkansas and from there driven across the state line west of Coffeyville and thirty miles east of Sedan in February.

In early May 1890, a meeting was scheduled at the Dennick schoolhouse in which Frazer and Gibson were invited. William Gibson did attend in an angry mood generated by the numerous written threats and whispers. He stated that their cattle were under control of the sheriff under quarantine and he was not willing to deal with mob hostility. Two nights after the meeting fifteen and three quarter miles of fence were cut beyond repair that bordered the Frazer and Gibson cattle.

A letter written by Presley Hale Gallion of Moline to Michael B. Crawford (whose father was Judge William Boyle Crawford of Girard) in Howard on April 28, 1890 caused quite a stir and continued to do so a year later. Gallion was a People's Party candidate for the Register of Deeds in 1890. The subject of the correspondence was the shipment of 18,000 head of Texas cattle to be placed in Elk and Chautauqua Counties, 3000 to be unloaded in Moline where the Elk County Committee was to meet the Chautauqua County Committee regarding safe delivery of the cattle. The cause for concern was another five miles of fence cut north of Sedan. The letter implied a lack of faith that the Elk County Committee would carry out their duties while the Chautauqua County Committee had to be in Sedan dealing with the damaged fence. Gallion made a point of stating the Alliance did not authorize the vandalism, but had a flippant air to it.

The Weekly Times Star of July 11, 1890 issued a correction regarding the reward. It clarified that the $1000 reward was for each offender, however many might turn out to be involved, and not just a flat $1000. Governor Humphrey posted an additional $300 per suspect to sweeten the pot. A general feeling that the sheriff would do little to apprehend the "villains" was denied by the newspaper, which fully supported the efforts of the sheriff's department in hunting down the killers.

On July 13, 1890 the funeral for John Frazer was held in Moline, Kansas at 11 o'clock in the morning with the Reverend William Clark Goodwin of the Methodist Episcopal Church in Moline facilitating. Goodwin was a Civil War veteran who served with the 92nd Regiment enlisting at Louisburg, New York in 1861. The service was well attended.

The memorial written by Reverend Goodwin for John S. Frazer took up nearly half a page and appeared right next to the article about the discovery of his coat and vest. Goodwin wrote a rambling, accusatory tribute to the slain stockman that reflected his high opinion of the deceased man.

"John S. Frazer was in the strength of a busy, useful, noble manhood, attending in a quiet honorable way to an honorable and necessary business, when he was set upon and killed by men he had never wronged by word or act and whose interests he would have served." The reverend of the Methodist-Episcopal Church also lectured the community on the fact that anyone hiding any information on the murder was an aider and abettor. He went on to talk of blood stains on the souls of the criminals and compared them to Pilate.

The residents of Chautauqua County, while disgusted with the homicide and frustrated with the law's inability to identify and arrest suspects, were also ready to close the case. Solving the case was proving difficult and expensive for the county and it appeared that those involved would merely cover for each other leading to no satisfactory outcome. However, Elk County residents were not ready to let it go.

On Sunday, July 20, 1890 the coat, vest and personal belongings of Frazer were discovered by Silas Walker and

Frank Hendricks two hundred fifty yards northeast from where the body was found as they searched for a missing cow. The men reported to Sheriff Sandy Lowe in Sedan who rode out to the scene with Elk County Sheriff Richolson who happened to be in town. The coat and vest had been carefully draped over the dead limb of a jack oak tree, which stood between two bushes. His gold watch was in one pocket of the vest and in another some silver coins. In the coat pocket was his cattle shipping book, receipts and a blank check book and handkerchiefs. Missing was a large wallet with two ten dollar bills. The shipping book was inserted into the coat pocket so that it could be seen sticking out.

On Wednesday, July 9, 1890 there had been a rain storm, so it was supposed that the items had been deposited at the location after that time since they had not been wet. Clearly, whom ever placed them there desired that they be found or they could just have been burned. The blood on the clothes was dry and bore signs of being under some heavy object as Richolson noted indentions from the watch chain on the vest.

As word got out a Pinkerton detective named, Charles M. Weber, hired a horse and buggy and rushed out from Sedan to the scene. Weber was Assistant Superintendent at the Pinkerton Kansas City station. He stated he had been engaged by the governor to investigate the murder. Detective Weber apparently forgot his badge, a fact the *Sedan Times Journal* noted with sarcasm. Weber met with Deputy Sheriff Ben Adams to discuss the case, but no record of the information discovered exists [7]. He left Wednesday, July 23, 1890 without finding any clues to return to Kansas City.

Six

The Elk and Chautauqua County Investigations 1890-1893

The main resources for the Frazer and Gibson murders that remain are the articles published by the newspapers of the time, most notably, the *Moline Republican* and the *Weekly Times Star of Sedan*. Most other newspapers carrying the story statewide merely reprinted from the two main sources. Like journalists of today, newspapers tried to compete with different details and facts to lure readers.

The murder also gave opportunity for revenge against spouses such as the arrest of Frank Davis in Independence, Kansas in July 1890 [1]. He was accused by his wife, Maggie James. Apparently their marriage was a dud from the start with Mrs. Davis receiving the blame when she left for Iola, Kansas. Her response was that she could not live with a man who could be involved in such a murder. When Montgomery authorities questioned her there Maggie retracted her accusations [2].

One such difference in reporting was in the alibi of Gray [3] who claimed to have spent Saturday, June 28 all day in Spring Creek at the post office leaving his house at 5 a.m. A Mrs. John Greer who was a neighbor of Gray's reported seeing him pass her house between 9 o'clock and 10 o'clock that morning on the way to Spring Creek. A neighbor, while visiting the Gray home, stated that Gray returned in a confused state of mind. When his wife inquired about his agitated condition, Gray replied that he was just hot and tired. It was after that conversation that Wilson Gray then actually went to the post office at Spring Creek telling people there that he might be suspected of something, but that he could prove his innocence by saying he was at the post office all day. He did not arrive until after 10 a.m.

The Moline Republican and *Elk County Citizen* also elaborated on the previous threats and cutting of wire fences that went unpunished by law enforcement. If such persons had been reigned in the murders may have been prevented and allowed Frazer and Gibson to make good on the losses suffered from diseased cattle [4]. The papers stated outright that the perpetrators were known and should have been arrested. It also pointed out that with both men dead and their estates having to be sued for recovery, that there would not likely be enough to pay much for any losses.

Support for John S. Frazer in Elk County was obvious, at least if one believes the glowing tributes made by the *Moline Republican*. The man was honorable and had no enemies. If someone did not want to do business with him, Frazer left them alone, which would have been hard to do in Moline with Frazer owning part of the hotel, bank, feed store and a large residential section. In the probate publication notice in The *Moline Republican* on July 10, 1891 regarding Frazer's estate as submitted by his brother, William, John owned the following real estate;

"The southwest quarter of section thirty-four, township thirty, south, range ten, east, and the west half of southeast quarter of section three, township thirty-one, range ten, east and north half of southwest quarter of section twenty-five, township thirty, south, ranger ten, east and lots one, two and three in block one Frazer's amended addition to Moline, and lots seven, either and nine in block three of the said addition as well as lots ten and eleven and lot one in block thirty-nine in the City of Moline."

The paper also found it out of the question that the Farmer's Alliance could have been involved in such a brutal, illegal act.

The *Cedarvale Star* provided additional description of the crime scene where the search party found a trail made by four men walking together about three feet apart as if carrying a burden. Footprints were also found by the pool at Deer Creek, but did not provide any useful information. Saturday afternoon around 4 p.m. the dogs owned by Arch Hammond whose land was west of the pool, began howling strangely and ran down through the field to the water [2].

Attention toward rancher, Wesley Best, began to heat up with rumors and misinformation from newspapers such as the *Grenola Chief*, which proclaimed that the state veterinarian had declared Splenic Fever to be the cause of wide spread cattle deaths. It also implied that cattle from New Mexico were becoming infected. *The Citizen* of Howard, Kansas addressed the issue of rumor regarding the alliances of Elk and Chautauqua Counties being involved in the homicides of Frazer and Gibson and also denounced any involvement with cutting and taking down fences and mob intimidation tactics [3].

The rather substantial reward for apprehension and conviction of the perpetrators encouraged two amateur detectives to push Chautauqua County Attorney McGuire to study the results of their sleuthing activities in September 1892. Samuel N. West and John P. T. Davis (his son Frank was accused of the murder by his wife) who lived in Elk City east of Moline were positive they had solved the murder in the persons of Hutton and Kimsey. Initially, McGuire was unimpressed with their report and refused to swear out warrants due to lack of evidence [4]. West had been the Senior Vice President of the Elk City GAR Post 128 in 1890.

Not to be put off, the two detectives travelled to Topeka where they told Governor Humphrey of their efforts to solve the crime, and about the lack of cooperation from local law enforcement to apprehend Kimsey and Hutton, two cattlemen living in Center Township in north central Chautauqua County and leaders in the Farmer's Alliance. They were in partnership with a Thomas Turner who was not a suspect. Humphrey listened to their pitch then persuaded Senator Snyder Solomon Kirkpatrick of Fredonia to review the file in Sedan. Kirkpatrick sent Lewis Hanback, a former Congressman to Sedan and he too found their theory lacking and went back home. Davis and West continued to pester the governor who was not pressured into perusing the case and basically informed the men they were a nuisance. Insulted that all authorities dismissed their findings, Davis and West did what many people today and that is turn to the media.

The majority of newspapers had no interest in the ramblings of amateurs who were clearly just after the reward money, but they did find an ear with the *Freeman's Lance*. The editor published all the letters of Davis and West and included a few editorials of its own accusing the Republicans in charge of protecting the murderers. After a period of reading this barrage, County Attorney McGuire fired off a letter refuting their claims, which backfired on him. It would have been better to ignore the rantings that give them credence with a response.

The two sleuths were backed by supporters of the *Lance*, the Alliance and the People's Party, which encouraged Davis and West both in their pursuit of Hutton and Kimsey, and in laying blame on Republican authorities for failure to solve the case. Interesting considering Davis and West were Republicans. The pressure worked and McGuire issued arrest warrants for the suspects for the June 28th, 1890 murder of John S. Frazer. It was assumed that McGuire gave in to the Alliance and the People's Party candidate, T.J. Hudson. The People's Party (or Populists) were a left wing group opposed to big business such as the railroads. The rates charged for shipping goods and livestock were a primary reason ranchers chose to drive cattle rather than ship by rail. So, Davis and West knew the Farmer's Alliance would be more inclined to listen regarding misdeeds of Republicans who tended to be conservatives favoring the railroads.

On Monday, August 29, 1892, Chautauqua County Sheriff Hartzell, rode out to Center Township with arrest warrants for Hutton and Kimsey then locked the two men up in the Sedan jail. The county hired two attorneys to assist McGuire in the prosecution, Snyder Solomon Kirkpatrick of Fredonia and John Downing McBrian of Sedan. Representing the defense were Luther Scott of Howard and later, Peckham and Beekman of Cowley County. Justice King set a hearing for Monday, September 5, 1892 leading to the sheriff and his deputies riding all over the country serving subpoenas, even as far south as the Chickasaw Nation [5].

The Kansas City Journal ran a story on August 30, 1892 about the investigations of Davis and West with colorful references to their sleuthing skills, even including an imagined exchange between Frazer and his killers, which was accompanied by a sketch of some forty men stabbing Frazer who was tied to a tree. Davis asserted that Frazer's murder was "atrocious" and "accompanied by extreme torture." The article stated the murder was planned and carried out by the Farmer's Alliance of Chautauqua County, this bit of information being the theory of Davis after his investigations [7]. He stated the conspiracy consisted of thirteen subdivisions of the Alliance. This statement caused friction between Davis and the *Lance*, which had supported his efforts. Davis made several attempts to sell his story, including to *The Advocate* and the *Topeka Capital*, before the *Kansas City Journal* accepted it. He had written up the story with pseudonyms until the real culprits were determined. A young man at the *Kansas City Journal* saw the story as an opportunity and sent copies to various east coast newspapers [8]. The story was published by *The New York Press* in New York City in August 1892 to get the scoop on *The Kansas City Journal*, which printed the "dummy" names instead of waiting as requested for the names of Kimsey and Hutton. *The Kansas City Times* of September 1, 1892 had it on "good authority" that every member of the Center Township Farmer's Alliance would be arrested for the murder of Frazer. All searches for the original article were unsuccessful both in Kansas and New York newspapers.

On the day of the hearing the courthouse in Sedan was packed full of citizens awaiting to hear the awful truth about the savage murder of Frazer. Justice King heard the case along with an associate, Frank Clark [6]. A multitude of witnesses provided information that while abundant, was already well known by the public and lead nowhere concerning the guilt of the defendants. The *Times Journal* in Sedan indicated that a prime witness (John New) did not testify, but failed to mention a name or the reason. The trial continued to Thursday at 6 pm, September 8, 1892. The testimonies presented much circumstantial evidence that seemed compelling, but no clear connections between any of it. McGuire received criticism for wasting time and money and implied that this was not an "infrequent occurrence." In fairness, McGuire was in a tight spot with his office and that of the sheriff being accused of covering up a homicide. With two men claiming to have substantial evidence and managing to obtain publicity, he needed to take some action. Trials are fact finding missions after all.

The influence of the media cannot be overestimated. The butcher of Frazer was horrifying and newspapers were the only source of news available aside from gossip. The public only saw what the papers printed, which many took as fact. People were upset over the murder and lack of justice, so when the fact that it might be a conspiracy was offered as a reason, McGuire had to respond. If nothing else, the trial cleared the names of Hutton and Kimsey, though did nothing to quiet the rumors of a cover up.

In a letter to the editor of the *Freeman's Lance* of April 8, 1892, John Davis and Samuel West defended their attempts to root out Frazer's killers and any accusations of wasting court time and money. Davis explained that they merely wished to find and prosecute those responsible and had no ulterior motives when he wrote to Governor Humphrey for assistance which he gave on July 11, 1891. By July 20, the two detectives were meeting with County Attorney McGuire about how to proceed with a preliminary hearing to sort out the evidence. It was only the lack of concern and response from Republican authorities that prompted such efforts.

Politics certainly did influence public opinion and actions before and after the murder of John Frazer. The issues of Texas Fever reopened wounds between farmers and the railroad owners as prior to the disease becoming a problem, driving cattle to save money was a viable option. Republicans who favored the railroads were becoming alarmed by the Farmer's Alliance, which was made up of the new populist, People's Party.

The Alliance was made up of those who invested in cattle by mortgaging land, using their savings or obtaining loans: common people who could not afford expensive rail shipping or loss of livestock to disease. Though the Alliance was not a political organization, the People's Party had many members who belonged to it. There was a meeting at the *Times Journal* in Sedan around midnight on September 20, 1892 of Republicans who wished to destroy the Alliance, which they planned to do by blaming the group for Frazer's murder. This idea was initially rejected as it might send some Republican's over to the new party, instead it was decided to infiltrate the Alliance with old order Republicans. So Republicans who were not already members of the organization would join to turn the tide until the populists no longer wielded any power. The strategy worked initially as the Alliance received many applications for membership requiring the forming of new lodges to accommodate members.

While some Republicans opposed such a tactic as blaming the Alliance for the murder, most at the clandestine meeting bought the notion that is was necessary in desperate times. The initial plan to infiltrate the Alliance had backfired as the group encouraged people to be proactive and educate themselves on law and government, which actually turned a large number of Republicans to the new party. Common folks were no longer willing to just be told how the world operates by the rich. Dick Roe, who ran for senator, stated that "the People's Party was a party of anarchists and murderers, I only need refer you to the murder of John Frazer" [9].

Seven

More Arrests in 1894

In August of 1894 John New landed in the Montgomery County jail in Independence for selling goods under false pretenses in Wilson County. It was a fancy way of saying that New stole cattle and tried to sell them to someone else. As he sat in the dank cell it occurred to New that law enforcement would like to hear the tale Will Leckliter told him, but only if it knocked some time off the long sentence facing him. The state of Kansas did not respond very kindly to cattle thieves. He began telling his fellow prisoners how Leckliter had enlisted his aid in tending to five horses that had carried the killers of John Frazer back to Elk County that Saturday morning. The five horses were in a barn near Grenola and New was to help take them to John Cox's barn where they would retrieve two fresh ones and a spring wagon and return to Howard. The story got better as New added various details such as how Best had met New, McBee, Theo Cox and Leckliter at the New place and passed out $2000 in payment for services. New was paid $100 for his effort [1].

Initially, according to New, it was Leckliter that told him how Frazer had been laid out and by whom on the way to Grenola. However, according to the *Sedalia Democrat* of August 29, 1894, New claimed firsthand knowledge that Frazer rode over the hill and into the canyon and came upon them unexpectedly as they were still planning the crime. Leckliter hit Frazer over the head with a club while he was still on the horse. John Cox pulled Frazer off his horse, Theo Cox struck him in the head with a club (a deviation from the first story or both men hit him), and then McBee stabbed him in the heart then cut Frazer's throat with a hooked blade butcher knife. All ten men then stabbed him. The knife was then concealed somewhere close. He made no mention of the gaping wound in Frazer's chest, but it was enough of a story to grab the attention of Sheriff Richolson and District Attorney Charles Luther McKesson. On August 13, 1894, Richolson swore out a complaint against Wesley Best, Theodore Cox, Mark McBee, William Leckliter, John cox and Elmer Cox before Justice of the Peace Charles M. Ellis in Sedan Township [2].

The sheriff of Chautauqua County and a few deputies rode up to Howard on August 21 and arrested McBee and Theo Cox. On the way back they stopped at Moline and arrested John Cox. Best was found on his ranch south of Moline in the afternoon and was placed under arrest then the three were taken to the county jail in Sedan. Richolson went to Indiana to capture William Leckliter and Deputy Sheriff Taylor, of Chautauqua County found Elmer Cox in southwest Missouri. So began the events that would turn the justice systems in the two counties into a three-ring circus.

When Chautauqua County Sheriff Samuel Treville Hartzell (Hartsel) and his deputies, William F. Steadman, Allen A. Wilson and Dan Stough arrived in Howard, the two lawmen entered the town very low key to discuss the issue of arrest warrants for Mark

McBee and Theodore Cox with Elk County Sheriff Patterson [3]. The two suspects were handcuffed and transported to Sedan. Also arrested were Wesley Best, John R. Cox, Elmer Cox and William Leckliter. The information prompting these arrests originated with ex-sheriff Oley Richolson of Elk County. There were rumors of six or seven residents of Chautauqua County also being arrested, but as of August 23, 1894 this was unconfirmed. Richolson, who never stopped working the case, traveled to Muncie, Indiana to apprehend Leckliter. All were held in the Sedan jail except for McBee, who was incarcerated in Wichita, Kansas and Leckliter who was jailed in Independence. The *Longton Gleaner* of August 24, 1894 also mentioned an employee of Wesley Best being extradited from New Mexico named Enos Stonebreck (Stoneback), a previous resident of Center Township in Chautauqua County, Kansas.

Elmer Cox was jailed overnight in Nevada, Missouri on August 22, 1894 by Deputy Taylor who arrested him in Henry County, Missouri where he was a farmer [4]. *The Kansas City Times* described Cox as a single and "fine-looking man, 35 years of age" [5]. Taylor took his prisoner back to Sedan by the Nevada and Minden Railway.

Richolson had a strange conversation with William Leckliter on the train back to Kansas, which prompted him to place John New in the same cell with him in Independence, Kansas to pull more information out of him. William Leckliter was working at a straw board factory in Muncie, Indiana when arrested by Richolson. Oley Richolson would later deny all accusations made by Leckliter as described in *The Weekly Times Star* of September 21, 1894 [6].

On Tuesday morning, August 21, 1894 in Yorktown, Indiana, Will Leckliter emerged from the outhouse to have Oley Richolson grab him by the back of his long underwear and shove him toward his house. On the way, Richolson informed Will that he was being arrested by the request of the Delaware County sheriff. Oley forced the front door open to an astonished young family just sitting down to breakfast. Leckliter was pushed to the back bedroom where he was allowed to pull on pants and boots, then was marched passed his family with his fly hanging open. Will threw his wife a bewildered expression as Sheriff Richolson prodded his prisoner out to a waiting buggy.

Mary Wells Leckliter held one year- old Chris while their three little girls huddled around her and cried. Nora, the oldest, was only six. William Harry Leckliter begged Oley to let him comfort his family before leaving, but Richolson was in no generous mood. Will was only glad that his in-laws, Reason and Adeline Wells lived close by, so Mary would not be without help. Leckliter wasleft at the jail in Muncie, Indiana while Sheriff Richolson telegraphed orders to arrest McBee and the Cox brothers. While he was there, Oley also telegraphed the papers in Indianapolis, St. Louis and Kansas City indicating that the men had been arrested and why. He told Leckliter that it did no harm to tell people they were under arrest and the reason for it. Will did not appreciate the publicity and told Richolson so.

At the train depot in Muncie, Will was shackled with a trace chain, which is used for draft horses. According to Leckliter, Oley then bought a gallon bucket and filled it with beer and whiskey for the trip to Indianapolis. By the time they passed the other side of Yorktown the two men had drank plenty of the mixture and Leckliter inquired who had sworn out the complaint against him. Leckliter gave a detailed description of the conversations between him and Richolson on the journey back to Kansas as described in *The Moline Republican*, September 5, 1894.

"That makes no difference at all Billy and you will find that out later. The Cox boys and Best have given the whole thing away, no mistake whatever. The evidence is positive that you helped kill

Frazer and the best thing for you to do, Bill, is to turn state's evidence. Think about it, you'll clear yourself of this mess and put big money in your pocket. We'll divide the reward and I'll send you back to that fine looking wife of yours with plenty of money. That would put those other rascals in the penitentiary where they belong." Richolson sipped another ladle of his liqueur and beer mix. Leckliter said nothing.

When the train stopped in Indianapolis, the sheriff filled the bucket again for the next leg of the journey. Oley bought a paper and showed it to Leckliter.

"Now Leckliter, ya know you done it and here it is in the paper." Richolson pointed to the article about Bill and the others. "Just turn state's evidence and I guarantee upon my word and honor, that I'll send you back home with plenty of money and you won't be hurt in any shape or form."

"I'd help ya if I could, Oley, but I don't know a damned thing about that murder." Leckliter could tell that the sheriff thought he was an idiot. Did he really believe that Bill would fall for that trick with the newspaper?

They arrived in St. Louis after nightfall. Sheriff and prisoner ate supper on the platform and Oley refilled the bucket once more for the meal. Before starting the trip to Kansas City, Richolson filled the bucket again. Bill had grown tired of the transparent effort to loosen his lips and not just a little nauseated from all the alcohol. Outside of Kansas City when the beer ran out Richolson ordered a "nigger" porter to fill it up and gave the man thirty cents. The two drank until arriving at the Lansing Penitentiary around eight in the morning. Bill was given the choice of staying in the jail at Kansas City or going with Richolson on business to Lansing. Not having a fondness for confinement, Leckliter chose accompanying Oley to the prison.

They walked past the stone quarry where several hundred inmates were already hard at work. Sweat ran down Bill's face as he hiked up the incline and watched the rocks being shattered with sledgehammers. Fine yellow dust hung in the air that filled the men's lungs and the sun cooked the ground around them. Guards with Winchesters stood somberly by, hats pulled down over their eyes as they waited for someone to make a wrong move.

Richolson, who could see Leckliter studying the scene, remarked, "Leckliter, would this not be a pretty tough place for you to be working?" He stopped to let the reality sink into Bill's head. "Now, Leckliter, if you turn state's evidence, there will no chance of you being here, but if you don't, you will be, sure as the rising sun!"

William Harry Leckliter didn't chose to comment as he followed the sheriff to the far end of the quarry where the rock was loaded unto wagons that were pulled by a large steam engine. They paused while the rock was loaded then followed the engine to where the rock was transferred to rail cars by the inmates. Richolson pointed out the guards with the Winchesters who made the twenty odd men strain with the heavy rocks.

"Leckliter, this is pretty tough ain't it?" Richolson didn't wait for an answer, but turned and started for the main gate to Lansing which appeared to Bill to be made out of the same yellowish rock as the limestone in the quarry. The sheriff left his prisoner with the gate guard then went inside the prison. The guard nodded to Leckliter and commented on the heat. Bill agreed that it was too hot a day to be standing around outside.

Of course, Bill didn't believe that Best had admitted anything. Leckliter intended to keep his mouth shut despite the nearly toxic level of alcohol in his system. He had a headache that seemed to line the top of his brain with needles and a queasy feeling in his stomach made a hundred times worst from the heat. Oley Richolson really was despicable. He was looking for a way to wow the voters and solving the Frazer murder would be a dandy prize. Bill knew none of the details of the murder or the people involved aside from Best, but he wouldn't tell if he did. Best was right, the politicians would hang themselves if everyone just sat tight.

Richolson emerged from the prison and walked toward Leckliter and the guard. The sheriff wore a vest that was parted by his pot belly and his blue shirt strained from the burden of all that weight. Oley took Leckliter's arm and led him into the main building where he left him with several officers while he went back out and chatted with guard at the gate. He wanted to know if Leckliter had said anything of interest and the guard replied, "No".

Richolson was beginning to lose his sense of humor and was rough with Bill when he dragged him back out to the gatehouse and left him there again. The guard, a man with gray hair and a gray face, took a big swallow of water in front of Leckliter who could taste the limestone dust in this mouth. The officer approached the weary looking prisoner in chains and brought up Frazer's murder.

"I know all those men who were arrested and I can tell you, the best thing you could do for yourself and your family is to turn state's evidence." He took another long drink of water. "Of course, it's none of my business, but it would clear you and stick to the other fellows."

"Sir, I know nothing about that murder except for the gossip I heard in the streets of Howard." Bill found himself turned over to another guard who spoke of the same thing, then Richolson returned. Both the sheriff and the gate guard tried to pry information out of Leckliter yet again.

"Oley, I just don't know anything that would help the state!"

"Leckliter! There is no use for you to lie about it! I know from the evidence that we have against you that you know all about that case." Richolson continued to speak to the guard for some time then took Leckliter across the street to a hotel for dinner. While Bill stood in the foyer trying to brush some of the dust off his clothes,

Oley brought him back out onto the porch to point out the hundreds of inmates being taken to lunch.

"Leckliter, that is pretty tough to be marched to and from every meal by the point of a gun." Sweat dripped down his jowls as he prodded his prisoner to break down. Bill simply observed the men in the distance and shook his head. Mercifully, Oley got off his case long enough to eat in peace. Afterwards they sat in the parlor of the hotel and read newspapers. Bill was just getting into an article about the railroads when Richolson hit the paper with his fingers making Leckliter jump.

"Leckliter, here they go with all the convicts back to work. Damn, I would hate to be in that fix!" Oley slapped his knee.

The day wore on slowly as the sheriff took Bill back to the guard at the gatehouse. The two law officers kept prying at Leckliter about the case. The convicts came out of the prison a dozen at a time and with each group Richolson would make a remark of some sort.

"This is pretty tough, ain't it Leckliter? You can save yourself all this misery if ya just turn state's evidence and confess the whole thing!" Again, Bill had nothing to say. Richolson, weary of his prisoner's stubbornness, took Bill past the stone quarry once more on the way to the train station. At three o'clock in the afternoon the two men caught the train to Independence. Oley was in need of sleep and tried to shackle Leckliter to the seat, but he refused.

"No, you ain't chaining me to no car as I haven't done anything wrong. We could have a wreck, then where would I be?" Bill could see that there were bags under Richolson's eyes and his cheeks were flushed from too much booze. "You can shackle me to you while you nap." Oley refused that suggestion.

Richolson turned his obstinate prisoner over to Squire Hensley who lived in Busby, so that he could nap. Hensley reached into his small suitcase to retrieve a pint of raw whiskey which he insisted that Leckliter drink. After all of the buckets of alcohol poured into him by Oley, Bill was not going to stand for anymore. Besides, he hated raw whiskey. Hensley also wanted to talk about the Frazer case and suggested that Bill turn state's evidence as McBee and the Cox boys had already given him up. Leckliter merely replied that he had nothing to turn in for evidence.

Just before dawn the train rolled into Independence. Sheriff Richolson was fed up with Leckliter and placed him in a closed cell where Bill spent the night soaked in sweat and fanned himself with his hat to move the stagnant air. That Friday, McKesson, the district clerk, paid Leckliter a visit. They sat in hard back chairs in the main room of the jail. Bill knew it was no social call, even though they had been friends in the past.

McKesson let out a breath. He wore a dark suit and appeared miserably hot. "Leckliter . . . I am sorry to see you here, but the evidence we have against you shows that you are guilty and there is no mistake about it, for the Cox boys and Mr. Best have given the whole thing away on you." McKesson leaned to one side and made eye contact with the prisoner. 'They said you was to take the horses and the boys were to go down in the spring wagon and you was to turn the horses over to the boys. Now, understand, we do not claim that you done any of this murder, but that the money was paid to you by Captain Best and you was to pay the boys and bring the horses back to them. You was to have three hundred dollars to deliver the horses to John Cox's stable.' McKesson wiped his brow with a white hanky.

"McKesson, I'll tell you like I told everybody else, I don't know anything about the case or where you got this information. Best never give me any money except for what he owed me in a poker game." Leckliter squirmed in the wood chair as his sweaty buttocks had begun to itch.

"Now, Leckliter, you know all about the case and if you will set your price, we will find the money for you and guarantee you, upon word and honor of a man, that you shall not be hurt, and we will send you back home with plenty of money." McKesson's voice grew more forceful and his glasses slid down his nose.

"Do you and Richolson work from the same script? I do not know anything!"

McKesson let out a breath in frustration. "I know that you know everything about this case! It's getting close to train time and I have to leave." He pushed his spectacles back into place and left. Leckliter was taken back to his stifling cell. The next day he was placed in the blind cell with New, then three days later, William Harry Leckliter was escorted to the jail in Sedan by Sheriff Hartzel.

The previous story published in Elk County papers in 1894 was disputed in affidavits from McKesson and Richolson stating that Leckliter lied about all events. Richolson challenged Leckliter's lawyer, Luther Scott, to retrace the steps from Muncie, Lansing and Independence where he could prove the whole tale was a lie. (Weekly Times Star, Sept 21, 1894)

John New confessed that he knew the entire plot to murder Frazer. New was known for running poker games, embezzling and rustling cattle. The poker games were attended local men including Best, Leckliter and a curious man named Berndt Olsen from Sweden who spooked people with his physic predictions. The two events prompted the arrests of the businessmen. Theodore Cox was a blacksmith from Howard, his brother John a hardware merchant in Moline and Mark McBee a druggist in Howard. A preliminary hearing was set for September 3, 1894 to hear evidence provided by the confession. He claimed that he was hired, along with the other five men, by Wesley Best to murder Frazer because he refused to move the infected cattle. New was hired to hold the horses of the assassins while they committed the deed. He also claimed to know how much they were paid [8].

About this time, McKesson, who previously had made his low opinion of the Pinkertons well known, contemplated opening his own detective agency with Oley Richolson as president, himself as secretary and John New as chief detective. Whether this was a real plan or *The Moline Republican* being sarcastic is not certain [9].

The Leavenworth Standard stated that after the major losses, Wesley Best moved to Nashville, Tennessee and then to Columbus, Kansas. This is an example of the confusion over who moved to Tennessee as the *Moline Republican* stated it was W.R. Best and his wife, Theresa who were from Blount County, Tennessee who returned to Tennessee after the murder. Wesley Best did live in a boarding house in Nashville for a time. The author contacted the relatives of William Riley Best who indicated that the family had no knowledge of William ever living in Kansas or anyone in their family named Wesley. The couple is buried in Wellsville, Blount County where he was a carpenter. He served during the Civil War in the Union Army joining February 25, 1862 as a Private, Company K, 5th Tennessee Volunteer Infantry. On October 1, 1862, he was commissioned as a 1st Lieutenant and honorably discharged June 7, 1865. On August 4, 1890 he applied for his disability pension from Tennessee. W.R. Best died May 12, 1897. The author could find no evidence of him ever living in Kansas or why the area papers knew of him at all.

The man arrested was actually, Wesley Best, from Staunton, Macoupin County Illinois where he was a miller. Best moved to Kansas around 1885 where he purchased 1200 acres of farm land in Chautauqua County. A fine two story brick house was built on the property, which later burned down. Best had been living in Nashville, Tennessee after helping his sons establish a flour mill in Columbus and was arrested while south of Moline checking on his property. He died June 28, 1904 in Howard, Kansas. There is no question that this individual suffered severe financial loss from infected cattle with his herd of seventy-four prized Herefords being nearly annihilated.

Chautauqua County Attorney McGuire wrote a second letter in September 1894 again addressing criticism regarding his handling of the Frazer homicide case [10]. He was responding to some person calling himself "Taxpayer." The newspaper clearly sides with the anonymous critic since he had more taxes that McGuire could hope to pay. It also pointed out that the "harangues" spouted out by local newspapers had been generated by his first letter in 1892 where he refused to name New at that time. *The Moline Republican* asserted that there was no reason to keep New's statement from the public then or in 1894. It alleged that the secrecy was to protect the incompetency of Sheriff Richolson and Elk County Attorney C.L. McKesson for previous false arrests.

A primary issue was that New could have testified at the preliminary hearing, but McGuire gave no explanation aside from the fact that New was incarcerated and that the county had important evidence that the general public did not need to know at that time. New did however testify at the trial, which Taxpayer found objectionable since New was a felon. McGuire also wanted to know how "Taxpayer" could be aware of just what New said and determine it was unreliable. McGuire had travelled to Lansing to interview John New and found his statement credible and was corroborated by other evidence. It seems clear that the anonymous accuser was defending the six men arrested and may have even been involved.

Taxpayer asserted that the county wasted money allowing Richolson to travel out of state to arrest Leckliter when he had no authority. McGuire retorted that Oley Richolson was authorized by Governor Lewelling to make the arrest and was fully entitled to be compensated for serving the warrant.

One of the witnesses to testify was Keenan Hurst of Howard, who was a member of the state board of livestock commissioners.

During the Civil War, Keenan Hurst enlisted for 3 years as a private August 13, 1861, and was mustered into Company K, 27th Ohio Infantry on August 18. Private Hurst was mustered out at Chattanooga, Tennessee, August 17, 1864. During the summer of 1890, a few weeks after the death of William Gibson, he accompanied John Frazer to examine dead cattle of Best and some of the other farmers from Tick Fever. He had been called to the area several times for the same complaint.

The two men rode down in a buggy to the Best ranch to examine the dying livestock and then went to the Gibson place near Moline where Hurst left Frazer around dusk. Frazer's saddle horse had been tethered behind the buggy. Hurst then drove home to Howard alone. The route home on the north and south lane was covered with high, thick hedges on both sides. Combined with the plant growth and coming darkness visibly was sparse [11].

Hurst had also received warnings and threatening letters, so he began carrying six shooters with one at the grip near his feet and the other tucked into the grip strap for easy access. He saw two men walking ahead of him keeping the same pace. Alarmed, Keenan drove with one hand while grasping a pistol in the other. As Hurst drew close the two men parted allowing the buggy to pass between them. It was then that a third man appeared, seizing the bridles of the team. His two accomplices pointed guns at Hurst instructing him to put his hands up.

Being overcome with fear, Hurst jumped from the buggy and landed near one of the assailants. He pushed the pistol into the man's chest and demanded to know what he wanted. The unexpected burst of bravery surprised the men, who ran off alongside the road into the darkness. Afraid to move for a time, Keenan Hurst listened as the sound of running footsteps faded away then ran down the lane after the liberated team and buggy. Since the horses had only trotted Hurst had no trouble catching them.

This testimony served to further prove conspiracy and danger to certain citizens such as William Gibson, John Frazer and John Colean, a partner of Frazer's in the Moline feed store who died suspiciously in 1891. Colean was a well-known butcher in Moline and Burden, Kansas. The feed store in Moline was also a butcher shop located at the Long Bell Company Old stand.

The reason John New's testimony was not heard at the arraignment on August 21, 1894 was that he refused to leave Lansing prison. The state had requested a continuance until September 3, 1894 until New could be transported as their case was based fundamentally on New's confession. Representing the state was County Attorney McGuire who was assisted by R. J. Hill and William. S. Fitzpatrick. For the defense were, Luther Scott, William B. Glasse (who later became a judge and state senator), John Marshal, Sol S. Long and Walter McCauslin. Glasse was also a Civil War veteran and lived in Columbus, Kansas in 1894, a very well respected attorney.

Warden Chase of Lansing prison, was expected to arrive with New, but instead a telegram was sent by Elk County Attorney C. L. McKesson (McKasson) to Fitzpatrick that the prisoner was refusing to leave. Chase was not willing to force the inmate to go to Sedan to testify. This was a shock to the prosecution who had interviewed New several times and taken a written statement. The information he provided was substantial enough to send the six suspects to trial, but without New's testimony the collaborating evidence would not be enough to convict. A decision was made to dismiss the case until further proof could be obtained.

The dismissal of charges inspired John H. Cox to write a scorching letter to *The Moline Republican*, Oct. 5, 1894 damning McGuire for his incompetence and "deviltry". He further called McGuire a fool and bet him one hundred dollars that he had no evidence at all. It was time to put up or shut up. Cox also blasted Richolson for swearing they murdered Frazer four years earlier. Again, the *Moline Republican* clearly sides with the six arrested suspects who are deemed innocent victims. The editor also stated that if McGuire was "looking for an airing" he could have it and printed the following threatening poem;

"To Colorado for irrigation

To Nebraska for starvation,

To Kansas for castration

Helen damnation

Pop administration

I'm going to my wife's relation

Please make no demonstration."

While the charges were dismissed, the men arrested had their lives altered or experiences strange occurrences. When Mark McBee was jailed he surrendered his pocket knife and left it there when released. On September 6, he found it on his desk in a back room of this store in Howard. McBee figured someone had tossed it through the open window. Will Leckliter, who was extradited from Muncie, Indiana found himself stranded in Sedan once released with no funds to return home. John Cox had just lost his young son a few days before being arrested based on the tales of "the most notorious liar in Kansas." The stated he would lose his store to creditors because of the whole affair [12].

The case goes dormant until 1896. The legal documents from 1894 are not available for reasons unknown.

Eight

March 16, 1896 at Sedan, Chautauqua County

March 16, 1896 at Sedan, Chautauqua County

In spring of 1895 John F. New was arrested in Wilson, County Kansas for embezzlement and held in the Independence jail. He had formerly lived in Howard where he was convicted of cattle stealing and incarcerated at Lansing State Prison. The reader will recall that New refused to testify at the preliminary hearing in 1894 against Mark McBee, Theo Cox, Elmer Cox and William Leckliter. The reason being that he wanted a full pardon for his testimony and location of the murder weapon. He seemed to have a change of heart in 1896 when he again let it slip that he knew something about the Gibson and Frazer murders after a conversation with Leckliter while they were in the hospital together. Leckliter had repeated a story about a death bed confession from Elmer Cox.

Elk County Sheriff Taylor arrested Mark McBee, still a druggist in Howard, William Leckliter, a whiskey dealer in Moline, Theo Cox, a blacksmith in Howard and James Burgess, who had been riding the line for the sheriff observing quarantined cattle. Burgess had not been arrested in 1894. County Attorney McKesson claimed there was new information obtained in winter of 1894 and pardoned New in exchange for his testimony. The legal documents from 1896 are available at the Kansas Historical Society and include arrest warrants, expenses and subpoenas.

The preliminary hearing was held in Sedan on March 16, 1896 where bail was set by Judge Jackson at $6000 for each defendant, none of whom could raise the funds [1]. Richolson was deceased by this time having died in 1895. The Chautauqua County Attorney in 1896 was Ellis McBrian, who along with Under Sheriff John William Taylor, received threatening letters regarding prosecuting the case and threats were made against New for testifying. McBrian was assisted by Charles S. Reed and W.S. Kirkpatrick. The courtroom and streets of Sedan were packed with citizens from Chautauqua and Elk Counties eager to hear the outcome of the hearing. Leckliter, Cox, McBee and New were represented by Luther Scott and McCosland. Burgess was represented by Reuben H. Nichols and Thomas N. King. In hearing journal entry from March 28, 1896 the times for oral arguments are given precisely; For the State: Fitzpatrick spoke from 9:45 to 10:30, McCosland from 10:30 to 10:50, Reed 10:50 to 11:45 and McBrian from 4:14 to 5:45 in the afternoon. For the Defense: Nichols from 1:30 to 2:52 and Scott from 2:52 to 4:15.

On the first day of the preliminary hearing the following witnesses were heard: Thomas P. Wynn, John Glenn, Mahala Gibson and John W. Goodell. Wynn, an employee of Wesley Best, testified that he saw Frazer the day before the murder, which was Friday, June 27, 1890 at the Best farm. He was riding in a buggy with his saddle horse tied behind accompanied by Lee McPheron. The purpose of the visit was to access the number of sick and dying cattle. When leaving the men went east at around eleven or twelve o'clock [2].

The widow of William Gibson, Mahala, testified that Frazer arrived at her place around noon with Lee McPheron who did not stay the night. That evening a man named Charley Lane stopped at the house for a drink of water and Frazer went out to the well to speak with him. That night she was alarmed by the behavior of the dogs "raving and tearing about all night." Frazer left the next morning, which was a Saturday around six o'clock in the morning for the pasture.

The third witness was John Glenn, who lived half way between the Gibson house and the pasture. He stated that he saw Frazer sometime after six Saturday morning heading in the direction of the field. Glenn spoke to Frazer who nodded in response. Shortly afterwards, Glenn started for Sedan and passed Jacob Neinan Carr, then he stopped by the Briggs house. While talking to Briggs an elderly man named, Herbold, approached in a cart headed for town. Glenn later passed observed the old man passing the sign post. When Glenn reached the sign post he met Captain Campbell, which was beyond the pasture. He arrived in Sedan around eleven o'clock.

The county surveyor, John Goodell, was the fourth to testify that first day. Goodell lived to the east of the pasture in 1890. He relayed how he had spoken to James Burgess after the event who told him that he had felt sick that Saturday and stopped to rest in the shade at Charley Binn's cabin in the southwest corner of the pasture. The cabin was abandoned by 1890. Burgess claimed that he arrived home about the usual time, however, Burgess's wife heard the conversation and corrected him stating that she had waited dinner for him and then went out looking for him. Frank Kenesson was also there at the Burgess house and witnessed the discussion. Goodell then told of looking down Hunter Canyon after his daughter, Lena, relayed hearing screams of someone in distress, but saw or heard nothing. There were also no cattle in the area.

The second day commenced at eight o'clock Monday morning in Crouse's Hall, which could better accommodate the crowds and lessen court interruptions. Lena Goodell was the first in the stand relating how she had heard two screams coming from Hunter Canyon where the two draws merge between eight and ten o'clock Saturday morning. She informed her father, John Goodell, who investigated but heard nothing.

Elvis Calvin McBrian, deputy in 1890 under Sheriff Sandy Lowe of Chautauqua County told how he was riding the border of the Frazer pasture the Tuesday after the murder when met James Burgess who stated he was sick. McBrian was riding fence under the sheriff's orders to monitor diseased cattle and only learned of Frazer being missing from Burgess. That Sunday he accompanied Sheriff Lowe and Burgess to the pasture to search for Frazer. Burgess stated that Frazer's mare had been found by his son, Frank Burgess, in the pasture with saddle and bridle.

Thomas Wynn was recalled to the stand where he stated the excitement over Texas Fever was intense and the road to the Best ranch was lined with teams of horses constantly. Wynn saw James Burgess at the Best place two or three days after Frazer's murder around six o'clock in the evening after Wynn got off work. Burgess was speaking with Best regarding money that was owed him. Several days before Wynn saw Frazer that Friday June 27, 1890, Jerry Hutton asked if Frazer had been to see Best about the dead cattle,

Wynn stated that he had not at that time. Hutton replied that they were all very organized in the area. They would wait a few days, but then if something was not done, "all they had to do was whistle and something would pop."

Next on the stand was Frank Burgess, son of the accused, James Burgess. At age 21 he seemed to not be able to recall whether Frazer was expected to be in the pasture or whether they were out of salt for the cattle, or what he had said in previous interviews, but six years had passed. Frank rode the line Friday, but did not recall doing it Thursday. His father rode it on Saturday, but Frank did it again Sunday because James was sick. He did remember finding Frazer's horse near the north gate with saddle, halter and reins hanging loose. The horse was taken to the Burgess farm, then James Burgess went to town to notify the sheriff [3].

Jacob N. Carr, a Sedan merchant, then swore that on Saturday the 28th of June he left around 8:30 in the morning for the Best ranch to try a fever treatment for sick cattle. On the way Carr went just west of the Frazer pasture and saw cattle grazing near the Binn cabin. He rode over to inspect them for ticks. The cattle were both in the building and outside in the shade. There were no other people in the area. Carr indicated that he had met a stranger he did not know just before and then between the cabin and King's place had met family of Joshua Greer riding in a wagon. After that he saw John Glenn at his farm around 9:30 am.

Frank Kenesson was recalled to relate the discussion he had with James Burgess with John Goodell present, regarding riding the line and stopping at Binn's cabin to rest in the shade. Glenn had claimed that he returned home at the usual time, but his wife disagreed.

Next to take the stand was the landlord of the Palace Hotel, John Cleveland, who after hearing his friend Frazer was missing rode with John Hansen to Sedan Sunday night June 29. The next morning they drove to the Burgess house for directions on how to access the pasture. Cleveland stated that he knew James well. That Saturday, June 28, Burgess told them that he had been sick and did not ride the fence. Cleveland and Hansen inquired as to where they should start looking and Burgess told them the waterholes to the west and informed the men about the north gate. They rode northward to search the road before other people came through the gate. Burgess later joined them in searching the western low ground, but then Burgess stated it was a waste of time and they should search further down [4].

John W. Hanson (George) a shopkeeper from Moline, verified the testimony of Cleveland in that Burgess stated that he had not ridden fence that Saturday and the best locations to search for Frazer. Hanson was a Civil War veteran with the 76th Illinois Infantry for four years.

William Riley Jones, who lived on the farm where Frazer's body was located, explained how he found the corpse near the pool while repairing fences around ten o'clock Monday morning June 30. He then informed the searchers in the pasture.

Next, former sheriff, Sandy Lowe, was cross examined regarding Burgess telling him about Frazer's horse being discovered. Burgess relayed that "old man Green" had told him of a saddled horse running loose in the field and he sent his son to capture it. Burgess only stated that it looked like Frazer's horse after they had returned from the pasture. Lowe had organized a search on a skirmish line plan, but the coat and vest were not found at that time. He was certain if the clothing was there the men would have found them. That Monday when Frazer's body was found no one rode the pasture line as Burgess had refused unless someone accompanied him.

Eli C. Ackerman was questioned regarding finding Frazer's hat at the end of the pool at Deer Creek where the body was found.

It had a bloody handprint on it. Ackerman had been a member of the search party. Ackerman owned a hardware store in Sedan.

Daniel Woodworth then testified that on June 28, 1890 rode along the east side of the Frazer pasture on the way to Sedan. When just south of the Goodell farm he heard a loud voice in the distance. Woodworth stated that the sound was west of him between ten and eleven o'clock in the morning [5].

Dr. Olney testified to provide an alibi for Theo Cox. He had previously denied all of John New's testimony and appeared nervous and hesitated in his answers when questioned on the inquest of William Gibson. Olney left the court room when Charles Reed of the prosecution denounced him. He was scheduled to testify the next week for the defense [6].

Nine

The Testimony of John F. New

March 17, 1896 Chautauqua County, Kansas

The much awaited testimony of John New had drawn a large crowd of spectators both in and outside the courthouse. New had been charged along with Theo Cox, James Burgess, William Leckliter and Marcus McBee for the murder of Frazer and had been given immunity for his testimony against the other men. The prosecutor was Charles S. Reed of Fredonia, Kansas. New was the last witness. For some reason that is not clear, Wesley Best was not charged with a crime, even though he was originally arrested for the Frazer murder.

New stated that he was thirty-nine years old and had spent two years at the penitentiary for "stealing somebody else's cattle".

He did not know William Gibson or James Burgess, but was acquainted with Dr. Franklin Olney, Mark McBee, Theo Cox and William Leckliter. He began his testimony by describing an incident with Dr. Olney at his drug store. New went into ask the doctor to help him "commit a criminal operation" on his wife. Olney agreed for a price of fifty dollars. New returned the next day and stated he did not have the finances. New was going to leave, but Olney offered an alternative method of payment.

Dr. Olney had accepted a proposition to take out two men by poisoning; they were William H. Gibson and John S. Frazer. New was to take the "medicine" to kill Gibson to Moline where he was to wait for further instructions [1]. He stated that he took the drug to Moline on the evening train May 20, 1890 and passed it off to a stranger. Concerned with being tied to the crime, New asked what effect the drug would have on Gibson and Olney replied it whisky and laudanum, which would make him drowsy and sleepy. The next morning while in Howard New learned of Gibson's death. That evening New saw Olney after the autopsy at the drug store. He inquired as to how things were going. Olney pointed to Gibson's stomach laying on the table and added that he was having a hard time convincing Dr. William H. Smethers that Gibson died from heart failure.

On June 26, 1890 New had a discussion with Dr. Olney at his drug store about killing a second man, John Frazer. New had no interest in directly committing homicide, but would assist in some other manner if it could be carried out after nightfall. That next day, a Friday, New agreed to help for one hundred dollars. He was instructed to contact Theo Cox, which New did at his blacksmith shop. Cox was making a knife when New arrived, so he assisted by inserting the handle and fixing it with rivets. One side of the handle was oak from an old plow handle and the other walnut from an old table leaf [2].

Theo Cox then told New they were going to start out at 2 o'clock from Grenola, a few miles west of Moline. The conspirators would be Theo, John and Elmer Cox, William Leckliter and Mark McBee, who would go by horseback to the Gibson schoolhouse. If New wanted to help they would leave a horse and saddle at John Cox's barn then he could meet them at the school house. After whistling twice, Theo Cox would come out and greet him.

After giving the signal Cox emerged and told New that the plan had fallen through as Frazer was at the Gibson ranch. New inquired as to who was in the school house and was told; John and Elmer Cox, McBee, Leckliter, Jones, Jim Burgess, Tom Turner, Frank Kimsey, Jerry Hutton and Wesley Best. The plan now was for Theo to accompany Leckliter and Burgess for an ambush in the pasture since it was known Frazer would be riding that direction to inspect cattle. Cox and Leckliter would hide while Burgess guided Frazer to the site. The rest of the men were to return to Howard.

That night New rode back to Howard with McBee and John and Elmer Cox. The next morning, Saturday, New saw Leckliter around 3:30 in the afternoon. He stated that they had their man and he needed to come to John Cox's barn that night. Elmer Cox then told him to meet Leckliter at the barn as they needed to move Frazer's body.

After dark the men lead three horses to the pasture. Near the pasture they went north on a road west of the fair ground, crossed a fence and tied up their horses just east. They then went north half a mile where they climbed a fence and crossed a ravine. When they came up on the corpse it was covered with weeds and a gunny sack. New pulled the knife from Frazer's body, took off the vest and rolled the knife up inside it. He then tucked the bundle inside his coat. It was sprinkling and the countryside very dark.

New stated that he took the hitch strap off his bridle and placed it around Frazer's neck, Leckliter placed his strap around the feet. They then hooked the straps around their saddle horns with a half hitch and carried the body between the horses to the creek. The brush was thick requiring them to back out once. New's horse then bucked, so he let the strap loose and the body fell. When the horse settled own New reattached the strap and they continued onward. It was there that they lost the hat. Once at the pool at Deer Creek the men removed the straps and rolled the body over the bank into the water [3].

New and Leckliter returned to the fence where they left the other horses then rode east to the road where Leckliter said Burgess lived. At the barn there they met three men, Jim Burgess, Tom Turner and Frank Kimsey. Leckliter had a gunny sack and tossed it on the ground says, "Jim there's that sack, better take care of it." The group returned to Grenola through Moline, the same route as before and retrieved a wagon belonging to John Cox and coats from the barn, one of which had a name tag with Mark McBee inside the collar. New went to Howard arriving around 11 o'clock Sunday. He then went to John Cox's barn.

That evening, New saw Leckliter at Olney's store where Leckliter told Olney that New had done everything he was required to do prompting Olney to pay the one hundred dollars owed. It was in an envelope marked, "No. 6".

On the night of July 3, 1890 New returned to the pasture to place the vest on a dead tree limb. He inserted the watch and some papers in the pockets, which included a telegram regarding cattle shipments. This was the only trip back to the crime scene. There was no cause for concern until July 1893 when Theo Cox went to see Powell in Severy. Powell indicated that he was making progress on the case when it was taken from him and given to a Pinkerton detective, probably Weber.

When John New was arrested and jailed for cattle stealing Theo Cox visited him offering to put up his bail. Cox would pay

$500 and Dr. Olney, $500. In exchange New would sign over his share of 120 acres of corn. He was instructed to jump the bond. New gave Cox the bill of sale for the corn, but never heard from Cox again. There was no bail out and New remained incarcerated. He would later be transferred to Lansing registered as inmate number 26557, New, John Fredrick. 1 6832 G 372 WL KS 3/1/1894 Embezzlement & Obtaining Money under False Pretense.

On cross examination New stated that he had never seen John Frazer until viewing his body. Oley told him that the two men that needed killed were from Chautauqua County. New had seen William Gibson at Moline because they had rode down on the same train. John had informed Olney when being told to take the drug to Moline that he, "Wouldn't do anything in a criminal way unless it could be done after dark." He had a family and was trying to get a new start in life. His pay for the delivering the drug was medicine for his wife and her needed surgery. Once in Moline New gave the half pint bottle of whiskey and laudanum to a man Olney called, Straight, waiting for him at the depot. He was a stranger to New so he would be wearing a red handkerchief tied around his right hand for recognition. The man hailed New who handed the bottle over to him. That was the end of the transaction for New who began walking back to Howard. In less than five minutes New saw Straight standing next to Gibson. He testified that he saw the man at Lansing, but was not sure since he was wearing prison stripes. New was probably right as there was a man named, Otis W. Straight, inmate number 35131 from Chautauqua County incarcerated in Lansing on 11/20/1894 for Grand Larceny. It was later determined that Gibson was given the whiskey flask by a chance acquaintance in Moline.

Regarding payment for the murder, New testified that Olney and McBee were to receive the money from Wesley Best on Sunday. Oley then sent New to Theo Cox that Friday to pay the others.

During the conversation with Cox, New was told that the original plan was to kill Frazer in Elk County, like Gibson, where Dr. Oley was the coroner.

New described the route and surroundings on the way to the Gibson school house and the trip to the pasture in exact detail including the distance between fences and other landmarks. The area was very dark and rained on New and Leckliter before they reached the school house. He testified that he took Frazer's vest to his cow barn, that the body had no coat. When New's horse bucked and he dropped the strap tied to the corpse it was near the creek. He then ran into the brush to avoid the horse kicking and dropped Frazer's hat about 150 yards from the pool.

The plan had been to keep the vest and gold watch in the event New and Leckliter were not paid promptly for their efforts in the crime. Once compensated, the men placed the items on the dead tree limb and arrived in Grenola just before daylight. After paying bills New and Leckliter rode onto Howard.

New first relayed his knowledge of the murders of Gibson and Frazer to Sheriff Hiram Sparks McCray, but without the details that would come later. At Lansing ex-sheriff Oley Richolson and Deputy McKesson pressured John New to make a more detailed statement about his knowledge of the murder. New testified that Warden Chase threatened to starve him if such a statement was not provided. McKesson and Richolson first questioned New at the Montgomery County jail in Independence, Kansas where he claimed that he requested an attorney. Richolson replied, "This is Populist fish we are frying and Populists are going to fry it, and you can't see any attorney."

All three men plied him for information once at Lansing penitentiary with McKesson offering $1200 of the reward money and Richolson would throw in another $300. The money enticements did not work either. William Leckliter was then brought up to Lansing where he tried for several hours to convince John New to talk, but he refused.

The Chautauqua County prosecutor asked New if he had requested a pardon at that time and it was refused and that was why New did not give a statement. New replied that he did not ask for anything, but refused to talk because they bribed him. He did eventually sign a statement after the warden threatened to withhold food. New signed the document for McKesson before a notary, apparently without reading it as he testified that he did not know what was in the statement until reading it in the Howard *Courant* and Moline *Republican*.

The prosecutor fired off, "You mean that you were bulldozed by threats of starving?"

New answered, "I was there under Populist administration, and I mean to say that they starved men to death right there."

After being pardoned for his cattle stealing crimes at Lansing prison, John New was immediately arrested at the prison door for the Frazer murder. He was not aware of this being part of the deal when he informed Chautauqua County Attorney McBrian of his knowledge of the murder.

Cross examination by the defense revealed more history of New's past and the crime. He testified that he had been in the patent right business and if he wanted to "do dirty business, he got Leckliter to help him out." The embezzlement charges could be related to this activity.

New elaborated on the scheme to finish up the murder of Frazer, whether that occurred in Elk or Chautauqua County. Dr. Olney told him that in order to receive their money the Frazer murder had to happen first. New had never been south of Moline. He again described helping Cox fashion the knife because Theo did not want to use a pocket knife as it could fold up.

Once at the Gibson school house New saw no one aside from Theo Cox. It was after they started back that the men ran into John and Elmer Cox and Mark McBee. They told New that Wesley Best, James Burgess, Jones (could not remember his first name), Frank Kimsey, Tom Turner and William Leckiter were already there.

Doc Olney said that the man named Straight lived in Chautauqua County and he had delivered three horses to Grenola; these were the same horses New would handle the next night. New had thrown the knife down between where he left the vest and the pool. He told the court that he next saw a knife at Lansing where McBrian asked him to identify it as the murder weapon, but New would not. He did supposedly admit it to a prison guard named, Hiatt. The murder weapon would not be found until August 29, 1899 around two hundred yards from the pool in Deer Creek where Frazer's body was found. The knife was found by a black man named, Frank Holt, who had been cutting corn for Cal Floyd. It was exactly as New as described John Cox making it; from on old file blade about ten inches long with a scabbard made of an old boot top. Blood stains were still on the blade and inside the scabbard [4].

Testifying after John New was Dan Barber who lived in Pawhuska, but in June 1890 he worked at the Grenola livery stable. He was a longtime acquaintance of Cox, McBee and Leckliter. Barber stated that two or three days before Frazer's murder, McBee, two of the Cox men, Leckliter and two strangers arrived at the stable around six o'clock in the evening. The two strangers were on horseback with each leading a horse behind them. The other men were in a two-seater spring wagon that contained two saddles in the bed.

The group then went to the hotel for supper. A short time later, the men returned for the horses and left around seven o'clock, leaving the wagon and harness at the livery. They left on horseback stating they were going to look at some cattle. The second morning after two men returned for the wagon around 9:30 or 10:00, but Barber did not remember who they were. He helped the customers hitch it up and then brought them coats that had been left in the stable. Mark McBee's name was in one of them. Barber knew this was before July as he had left the area by then. He added that he did not know the two men that came on horseback or the four in the wagon.

Next on the stand was Edgar Chill who had rode fence for Chautauqua County Sheriff Lowe for four or five months before Frazer's murder. Chill, who was a manager at the Burgess barn, discovered a bloody gunny sack in the barn in July. He had business with Burgess that day and turned his horse loose in the corral before going into the main house. When entering the barn to fetch the horse he saw the sack either rolled or wadded up, bloody and mildewed. A few days later the sack was gone.

Chill testified that he received threatening letters, which he tore up thinking it was a joke. The first of the letters was regarding his riding the fence and the last was sent after Chill moved to Pawhuska warning him to "go slow about any knowledge I had or I might disappear as Frazer and Gibson had." The letters were signed with twenty marks instead of signatures and the letters seemed to be written by different hands.

The last witness that Tuesday was Freddy Loyd, twelve years old who identified the knife he found near the pool. His cousin, Harry Loyd, who was with him verified it.

Ten

Further Testimony on March 18, 1896 Chautauqua County, Kansas

The first on the stand that Wednesday, March 18, 1896, was Harvey Pierce Moser [1]. He had discovered a trail from the location in Hunter's Canyon where the murder was assumed to have occurred to the pool at Deer Creek where Frazer's body was found. It had been formulated earlier in the investigation that Frazer probably stopped at that place because there was a spring there and it was an easy area to cross the stream. The trail was created by horses, but he did see a man's footprints in the draw where it looked like someone had ran into brush and then backed out. This would collaborate New's testimony.

Jacob Neinan Carr, then described an area where the weeds had been cut and the ground appeared as if two persons had lain there. There were also impressions of something heavy being placed in the area.

Testifying regarding the wounds to Frazer's body during the inquest of 1890 was Dr. Milton Trowbridge Evans of Sedan, Kansas. He stated that the cut across the throat was from one side to the other and the windpipe nearly severed. The main jugular vein was not severed. The wound was ragged [2].

Evans testified that there were seven stab wounds in the left breast around the nipple with the principle incision penetrating the heart, which would have been immediately fatal. In the abdomen were four wounds with one penetrating the abdominal cavity. Evans noticed a blue ridge around the back of Frazer's head, which was made before death. The doctor did not think the strap around the neck could have produced that mark. This would tend to validate theories that someone waited for Frazer to show up at the spring and then ambushed him, maybe striking him from behind.

Dr. John M. Sharpless, who was also at the 1890 coroner's inquest, took the stand and described the wounds as fatal. He was puzzled by the abrasion on the back of Frazer's head and neck. The skin was peeled off with some discoloration, but no swelling. Sharpless stated that he still could not explain the wound. Odd, since New stated that Frazer was clubbed on the back of the head and the body later dragged to the creek. The wounds seemed to make sense.

To testify against the reliability of John New's testimony was Ike Hudson, the postmaster of Fredonia, Kansas in Wilson County where New was living when arrested. He stated that before being incarcerated for cattle stealing New's reputation had been good. After that New was seen as a bad person. A Mr. J.A. Cooper, also of Fredonia, verified his testimony.

Dan Ellis, a laborer who lived between Moline and Howard in 1890 related how he met Theo Cox and William Leckliter on the road north of Moline the day of or before Frazer's death. They emerged from an eastern lane and turned south just ahead of the road and direction Ellis was travelling. Cox and Leckliter were on horseback and spoke to him around ten or eleven o'clock. At his point the state rested and the defense placed James Burgess on the stand.

After a few introductory questions, the court learned that Burgess had lived in Kansas since 1880 in Center Township near Wesley Best where he was into farming and ranching. Prior to living in Chautauqua County, Burgess stated he had resided in Barber and Lynn counties in Kansas and in Colorado and Saint Claire County, Missouri. Around April 1, 1890 he moved into the Binn house to the southwest of the Frazer pasture as an employee of Gibson and Frazer. His first task was to repair a half mile of fence that had been cut. There were 800 head of Texas cattle in the pasture and it was his job to tend them and watch the fence. The wire cutting had started prior to Gibson's death. The cuts were made between the posts and all three strands [4].

The usual schedule required riding fence daily. On the Wednesday, Thursday and Friday before Frazer's murder James did not perform that duty due to illness, his son, Frank Burgess worked on those days. On Saturday, James rode fence to allow Frank to plow the corn as he was still sick and had fallen behind. Starting off at seven o'clock in the morning Burgess saw no one until on the west side of the pasture. He did not stop except to occasionally place a few staples in posts, then went to Charley Binn's cabin in the southwest corner of Frazer's pasture to rest in the shade for twenty-five to thirty minutes. Fred Herbold, who lived at

Summit, Chautauqua County, came down the road and stopped to talk for a time with Burgess. He saw passers-by on the way home around eleven o'clock on the road that he did not recognize.

Burgess had not seen Frazer since two weeks prior to that Saturday when he was killed. That afternoon James went to Sedan to the fairgrounds to see a horse race around two o'clock. An explanation for the bloody gunny sack was that Burgess had a pony with a knife cut on its neck that hemorrhaged profusely, putting the animal's life in danger. The sack was used as a bandage until it was soaked and he replaced it. The horse was injured just before the death of William Gibson on May 23, 1890.

In responding to questions, Burgess stated he had not met Leckliter until a week prior to that Saturday of June 28, 1890 in Ellis' office in Sedan. After hearing John New's testimony Burgess denied all of it and stated that he had never seen the man until the day before in court. The reason Burgess went to the Best farm a few days after Frazer's murder was that Wesley owned him $200 for a loan, which was paid back that day. On Sunday, when his son Frank found the saddled horse running loose, Burgess recognized the black mare as belonging to John Frazer and rode to Sedan to notify the sheriff. The anger over Tick Fever was well known and James found the incident suspicious.

The prosecutor, McKesson, redirected, inquiring as to whether Burgess knew Theo Cox. He answered that he did not, nor did he know any of the Cox brothers. McKesson countered by asking the name of Burgess' mother. James replied that it was, Melinda. The state asked for her maiden name and James supposed it was "Cox" after first replying with the name, Burgess. James elaborated that she was raised in Gasconadeco, Missouri and as far as he knew was not related to Theo Cox. His mother did have a sister living in St. Claire County, Missouri named, Kimsey. He admitted that Frank Kimsey was his cousin.

James Burgess never saw Theo Cox until his trial, and did not see him when arrested before in 1894. James was in Sedan the day Cox was released then, but did not go with Kimsey to congratulate him at the Bryan Hotel. He added that Jeramiah (Jerry) Hutton was his wife's cousin. Frank Kimsey and Jerry Hutton both lost cattle to the fever and often stopped by the Burgess house. It was from them that James knew of the angry discussions about Texas cattle at the Farmer's Alliance meetings as he did not attend them.

Burgess had no idea that John Frazer was in the pasture that Saturday and made a statement to Pinkerton detective named Weber regarding it. Once again James repeated the activities he did on Saturday, June 28, 1890 in which he mended fence at the draw. The next time he saw Frazer was at the pool at Deer Creek when the body was found. He reached the cabin between nine and ten o'clock that morning, feeling sick like the day before on Friday. Burgess stated he did not say he was in the cabin as claimed at the inquest nor he stay there for an hour.

Frank Burgess brought Frazer's horse back to their farm around ten o'clock Sunday morning. James testified that he had been told by Joe Gibson (William Gibson's son) that if "anything came up to notify the sheriff, not get word to him." He supposed by that statement something was amiss with Frazer. Burgess did not tell the sheriff that old man Green had told him of Frazer's horse being loose in the pasture or that he sent his son, Frank, after it. Green may refer to a man named Finis M. Green who lived in Center Township in Chautauqua County in 1890 though at fifty he was not that elderly.

Burgess further testified that Tom Turner and Frank Kimsey were not at his house on Saturday or Sunday, day or night. James rode home from Sedan Saturday night near dusk and slept well with no disturbances. He thought that he had seen Kimsey at Sedan and invited him up, but he was not able to visit.

In response to John Cleveland and John Hanson stating that Burgess told them to search the creek pools or down below, Burgess denied it. He only recalled meeting them in the pasture Monday, June 30, 1890 and telling them he was not in the pasture that afternoon to inspect the cattle as he did every few days. Burgess denied saying that he did not ride fence at all. He then described his activities on Tuesday, in which Burgess made the rounds of men who owed him money staring with Wesley Best at $200. The next stop was the homes of Enos Stoneback (Stonebreck) and Richard (Dick) Speed in Center Township. Burgess was not sure if he had left Monday evening or Tuesday morning after previously stating he had spent the night at home on Monday.

Richard Speed Jr. accompanied Burgess on Tuesday morning to collect $75 due from Stoneback, but did not get it. He stated Turner and Kimsey owned him $500, Jerry Hutton, $250 and his own brother, $150. All the loans were due and James was attempting to collect those debts the two days after Frazer's murder. Turner and Kimsey repaid their debt in cash and cattle after Burgess moved to his present location in spring 1891. The state asked Burgess if he had $1200 in addition to what he loaned to Wesley Best and he replied that he did not and did not expect to have all the money paid back.

Luther Scott, for the defense, pondered that if Frazer left the Gibson place around six in the morning then he would have been at the pasture gate around eight o'clock and Burgess agreed. He then asked Burgess if he thought Frazer had been murdered and he replied, "Yes, I always said that I thought that he had been killed. I knew on Monday when Frazer's body was moved. Goodell and Jim Cannon came to my house that day. Didn't tell them that I wasn't going or that I had enough of it. Don't remember Cannon telling me that I better go, that I would get into it if I didn't. Didn't stay at home until I was called for, went to town (Sedan)". Burgess added that he did not ride the fence on Sunday or Monday, but did afterward a week later. He told the sheriff that he would never ride alone again.

Sarah Burgess, the wife of James Burgess, next took the stand to testify regarding the pony with the knife cut and the bandages. She provided details on who rode the fence lines on the days in question in 1890, meaning her husband and son. Sarah was positive that James returned home between eleven and twelve o'clock Saturday and they had no company at their house that night. James had been to the horse races that afternoon, but remained at home that night because he was sick. She had never seen the defendant, Cox, until in the courthouse hallway. Silas Walker and William Jones both recalled how they had seen the gunny sack bandages on the pony three or four weeks before Frazer's murder, confirming Sarah's testimony.

A young man named Ellis (Ells) McGrew testified that he had lost a knife near the pool where the body was located. He described it as doubled edged with one edge ground off except at the point; poor workmanship, but McGrew thought it was factory produced. The handle was made like a case knife in two pieces. The blade was four or six inches long and McGrew had possessed it for over four years before losing it. Ellis bought the knife from a boy. It was an old knife when he obtained it. His wife, Lillie, also described the knife and identified it, along with her sister-in-law. Lillie's father was Richard Speed. He had lost it while on a fishing trip to the creek the previous March or April (1895).

When Frank Kimsey was called to the stand he stated that he was not at the Burgess place on the date in question (June 28, 1890). Claimed he had never seen John New until taking his place on the witness stand. That night he stayed in Sedan at Harry Turner's house with Tom Turner. He went there after they had turned in at nine o'clock. Friday night he stayed with Edward. H.

Hughes as he was on a cattle buying trip. On Saturday he went to Chris Young's place and traveled with Hughes who went to town while Kimsey went to Young's to inspect a heifer. After that Frank had dinner at the Jacob Lantz residence. The remaining defense witnesses were called to provide alibi's for McBee, Cox and Leckliter and were from Elk County.

The Weekly Times Star of March 20, 1896 stopped the presses to announce that Justice Ellis decided to bind over for trial Theodore Cox, Marcus McBee, William Leckliter, John C. New and James W. Burgess for the first degree murder of John S. Frazer on June 28, 1890.

Eleven

The Trials Begin 1895 and 1896

The first trial of State vs. James W. Burgess, Theo Cox, William Leckliter, John C. New, Mark McBee and Franklin Olney was held at Fort Scott in a change of venue that resulted in a hung jury in summer 1895 [1].

On September 2, 1896, Burgess requested to be tried separately and it was granted. He pled not guilty. On Wednesday, the venire for thirty additional jurors commenced in Sedan. The state questioned the potential jurors carefully regarding their ability to objectively hear the case, a valid point since the venue had been changed twice. First to Fort Scott and then to Eureka where the trial for McBee, Cox, Leckliter and New was held. The prosecution particularly inquired as to whether jurors had any prejudices against those bringing Texas cattle into the county in accordance with the law, which might have brought Tick Fever to the area. The defense objected to the question, but was over ruled by the court [2].

The jury was emplaned Wednesday, September 1, 1896 at 11 o'clock and consisted of the following men; James Reynolds, Everett E. Turner, Samuel G. Shirk, Iain N. Drake, Charles A. Dale, John Wilkinson, John Chittendon, James W. Uhls, David Franklin Arbaugh, James Tolson Botts, and J.W. Laverly. The regular jury panel was not exhausted, so no alternates were required. It was noted that seven of the jurors came from the Cedarvale area and four from the Niotaze area, assuming the last one was from closer to Sedan.

The trial began Wednesday afternoon in the opera house in Sedan as the crowds expected were too large for the courthouse. Representing the state was County Attorney Ellis McBrian with Charles S. Reed of Fredonia and Hill, Fitzpatrick and McGuire of Sedan as co-counsel. For the defense was Reuben H. Nichols, assistant counsel, Thomas Napoleon King and Thomas J. Hudson.

The first witness was John Goodell who recalled the same information as in the preliminary hearing in March 1896. He described the Frazer/Gibson pasture where the murder was committed, the parties who passed by his place and the screams heard on the morning of June 28, 1890 in Hunter Canyon. Goodell testified regarding the route Burgess usually rode the fence line and that he had seen James Burgess at the pool in Deer Creek when the body was removed and then again later that day in Sedan. Burgess told him about riding the line Saturday and arriving home around the usual time, but his wife corrected him stating that lunch was waiting for him when Burgess returned home [3].

Legrand B. McPheron, Harriet Gibson and her son, Joseph, along with Mrs. Mahala (Gibson) Ahrburg took the stand to testify that John S. Frazer spent the night at the Gibson home that Friday night, June 27, 1890 and that he left early that Saturday morning for Sedan through the pasture. The family was disturbed during the night with barking dogs prompting Frazer to go to Joe Gibson's room around two o'clock and ask for a firearm. Friday evening at 9 o'clock Charley Lane stopped by for a drink and Frazer went out to the well to speak with him.

Keenan Hurst, who was a member of the Kansas Livestock Commissioner's Board in 1890, told the court how he had been stopped on the road by three men when returning from the Gibson place in Moline where he had gone with Frazer. The men said Hurst was not the man they were looking for and let him go.

John Glenn, who lived on the road between the Gibson place and the pasture, recalled seeing Frazer pass his house that Saturday morning.

Next on the stand was John Lovitt, who was a member of the GAR W.H. Gibson post at Leeds, Kansas. He stated that he rode south along the east side of the pasture that Saturday morning and saw a man on horseback to the west of Hunter Canyon riding down the slope toward it. Lovitt was repairing a wagon wheel east of the Goodell farm and saw two parties pass him. A man on foot walked to the south. This was between nine and ten o'clock [4].

Daniel M. Woodworth (originally born Glascow, but changed it after running away from home in 1859), a Civil War veteran testified that he heard a cry for help in the pasture between nine and ten o'clock Saturday morning. Lena Goodell also verified this.

Telling the jury about how James Burgess informed him of a loose horse in the pasture near the area where the murder was supposed to have occurred was Sandy Lowe who was Chautauqua County sheriff on 1890. Lowe had been a 2nd lieutenant in the Union army in the 7th Missouri S.M. Calvary. He then accompanied Burgess to the pasture where James told him that he knew of the horse from Green and that Joseph Gibson had told that if anything happened in the pasture to notify the sheriff. Frazer's name was not mentioned until they were headed to the pasture. Burgess stated that he had rode fence the day before after having his sons plow the corn in a field west of where they lived and he had ridden west of there on his route around the fence. Lowe added that a detailed search was made of the pasture and that the coat and vest were not there and were placed at the scene afterward.

The man who found Frazer's body, William Jones, who lived on the Roe farm in June 1890, a half mile northwest of Burgess, testified that he found the corpse in Deer Creek June 29, 1890 on Sunday morning.

Dr. Milton Evans and Dr. John Sharpless described again in detail the results of the coroner's inquest of 1890; seven or eight wounds in the chest area over the heart with two stab wounds in the abdomen. His throat was cut severing the windpipe. There were discolorations and abrasions on the back of the head, shoulders and neck. Sharpless added his opinion these wounds were made postmortem [5].

Members of the search party, Harvey Moser and Jacob Carr and others, told of finding areas of grass in Hunter Canyon where it appeared people had cut the weed and lay hidden. Carr stated that he had been at the Binn cabin between nine and ten o'clock that Saturday and no one was there.

On the second Sunday after the homicide, Silas Walker, described how he found Frazer's coat and vest about 300 yards from the Deer Creek pool.

Recalled to the stand was, Harvey Moser, who testified regarding finding a trail in the Arch Hammond pasture that lead from the north fence to an old road running towards the pool. The trail was made by two horses about three and half feet apart. Moser also saw the coat and vest, the vest appeared to have been rolled tightly leaving the imprint from the pocket watch chain on it.

George Hanson and John Cleveland of Moline described being at the home of James Burgess the Monday morning after Frazer was known to be mission. He gave them directions to the pasture and advised them that searching along the creek would be the best place to find the missing man.

James M. Brown, who lived half a mile west of the Gibson pasture, testified that while out checking his horses he saw a man sitting on the north side of Binn's cabin with a horse grazing nearby on the morning of June 28, 1890. On his way to town he saw the same man riding north along the fence. When Brown approached he saw that it was James Burgess and he was stapling fence to the post. Brown inquired as to why he had been sitting at the cabin and Burgess replied that he was sick. This was around seven o'clock in the morning. He stated that Clarence Anderson and Bud Baker had been with him. On cross examination Brown stated that he had not provided this information at the time because of talk that he would be arrested for cutting fence around the Gibson/Frazer pasture. Willis Edmund (Bud) Baker would collaborate his story when on the stand.

A booking agent, Henry Oliver, testified to meeting Burgess the Saturday morning of June 28, 1890 on the road running west from the Burgess house. He was riding a gray horse and travelling west.

Taking the stand next was Joe Gibson who told of two horses lent to Burgess by his father William for riding the Gibson/Frazer fence line. One was a chestnut sorrel gelding that was never returned or accounted for and was said to have strayed off.

On Wednesday the pardoned convict, John F. New, took the stand to testify and his story was much the same as at the preliminary hearing, except for a few evidentiary points. He recalled how his initial connection with the Frazer murder was through Dr. Olney who gave him a medicine bottle to pass to a fellow named Straight at the Moline depot in May of 1890. Straight was to be wearing a red handkerchief around his left hand, so New would recognize him. This differed from earlier statements where New said the handkerchief was tied around his own right hand [6].

On June 26, 1890 Olney asked New to assist with killing Frazer, which he finally agreed to do for $100. The initial plan was to ambush him near the Gibson school house and New was to meet the three Coxes, Leckliter and McBee there that Friday night on June 27, 1890 who would come by way of Grenola. However, they failed to get Frazer there so New was informed of a new plot requiring himself, John and Elmer Cox and Mark McBee to ride to Howard that night. Theo Cox and Leckliter would remain behind so that Burgess would direct Frazer to the pasture in their direction for the murder. The next day Leckliter told New that they got their man and that New was to accompany Leckliter to the pasture that night to get rid of the body.

New described going the pasture with the extra three horses the men had rode home the night before. They entered through the Roe place with New explaining the route taken, finding the body then carrying it to the pool as he had during the preliminary hearing. New and Leckliter returned to Howard via Grenola where they retrieved the team the Coxes and McBee had used for the trip to the Gibson school.

New explained that the arrangement was for McBee, the Coxes and Leckliter to go to the Gibson school house through Grenola starting on Friday afternoon, June 26, 1890. New was to ride directly to the school on horseback and meet them there. McBee and the Coxes left the wagon at the Grenola livery and took three horses from the stable for the trip to the school house.

On cross examination John New mentioned a name he had not before when going to the pasture with Leckliter to move Frazer's body. When testifying this time he stated that William Jones and Leckliter laid down the fence. New claimed that he did not mention this in the preliminary hearing because he was not only to give enough information to bind the parties over for trial. The men did not enter through the gate, but through the fence to the right. He also stated that he had not seen Jones before that day when he accompanied New and Leckliter down through the pasture. They tied the three extra horses to the first fence they went through. Both the first and second fences crossed were left down. Jones walked and guided them to where the body was located in the pool. He them left the other two men to deal with Frazer's remains. New carried the hat in his hand and placed the gunny sack on his saddle, sitting on it. The knife was rolled up in Frazer's vest and tucked inside New's own vest. When carrying the body their horses were between eight and ten feet apart. New stated that he never saw Jones again after that day.

The prosecutor interrogated New regarding the statement he had made to McKesson at Lansing Prison. He denied having dictated or read the statement and only signed under pressure from Warden Chase before the clerk of the court. New understood that when transported to Independence, Kansas that it was to testify against Cox, McBee and others, but refused to do so with a pardon.

The defense questioned New regarding the vest and he explained that he kept it until receiving his $500 from Dr. Olney. He found the wad of money wrapped in a check after returning home along with a gold watch and silver coins. New kept quiet about the cash as he wanted to keep it, but eventually gave Leckliter half a day or two day and prior to the vest being hung on the tree. New added varied details regarding the money, Jones being involved and the wearing of the red handkerchief at Moline. He explained away the handkerchief story by stating that he and Straight had both worn one.

Daniel Barber testified that on June 27, 1890 Mark McBee, Theo and Elmer Cox stopped by the stable to leave their team for feeding while going to supper. They left on horseback. Barber was familiar with all three men and positive it was them that day.

Countering New's testimony about McBee, Cox and others leaving Howard for the Gibson school house via Grenola on Friday June 27, 1890, Richard S. Blair of Howard, stated that at that time, Mark McBee and Elmer Cox were at the same stable as Blair hiring horses for a fishing trip to Caney. Around 2 pm Blair saw Cox's team leaving with four men in the wagon [6].

Stephen Mahrun of Elk County, stated that he went to Howard to have a plow sharpened, but the Cox blacksmith shop was closed and he never saw Cox that afternoon.

Richard (Dick) Gibson, third oldest child of William and Harriet Gibson, of Center, Chautauqua County, testified that he stayed at the home of George W. Satterlee on the Grenola and Gibson road that Friday night on June 27, 1890 when Frazer stayed at his mother's house. Around midnight he saw five men on horseback travel pass heading toward the Gibson school house.

The state rested its case Thursday afternoon and the defense began to examine witnesses. The first was James Burgess whose testimony did not differ from that of the preliminary hearing. When the Weekly Times went press Friday morning September 4, 1896 the defense was still presenting witnesses, but Burgess was eventually acquitted.

After the trial of Burgess, Nicholson filed another affidavit for change of venue citing the hearings of 1894 and the rantings of H. G. Mosier, who had spoken to crowds in Chautauqua County about the murder of Gibson by Dr. Olney. Mosier had become violent and was angry when accusing Olney of murdering Gibson and being involved in Frazer's murder. This behavior was observed in both Elk and Chautauqua Counties. When confronted with this information in 1894, Mosier stated that he knew nothing about the crimes and only reacted in anger when the defendants were released. Nicholson also referred to the Pinkerton detective, Weber, sent by the governor who had made all attempts to cause disorder regarding the case and assuming guilt.

In the affidavit filed by Nicholson in 1896, he also described the actions of Undersheriff Taylor who had traveled to the Oklahoma Territory with him on the same train seeking witnesses for the State. He had submitted substantial billing for these searches, but without providing a single name of persons interviewed. Nicholson mentioned that he was going to interview the Aukborn family and Tom Turner and Taylor replied he was going to see the same people. When asked who else he was going to see the Undersheriff would not answer. They were searching for people had lived near the Frazer/Gibson pastures in 1890. Taylor also stated that the majority of people in Chautauqua County felt the authorities had the right suspects. (Affidavit filed 1896 in Chautauqua County District Court).

On November 19, 1896 the trial of Theo Cox, William Leckliter and Mark McBee ended with acquittal in Eureka, Greenwood County, Kansas. The charges against Olney were dismissed and he was not tried. The testimony of witnesses was much the same as the previous trial of James Burgess and the preliminary hearing in Sedan in March 1896 with no new evidence presented. The defendants were represented by Reuben H. Nichols. The members of the jury were; Royal Wolcott, Elgeva V. Horton, John D. Mitchell, Robert Bruce Wolf, S. Schaffer, Jacob Jeigler, John H. Cochran, J.B. Mahon, H.J. Kesten, A.L. Manlin, George L. Baley, R. Mattingly.

The testimony regarding the knife found in the Floyd pasture was probably one of the most compelling for the various juries and the reason for the hung juries and eventual acquittals. The young Floyd boys stating the knife was theirs provided reasonable doubt in a case with little real evidence and perhaps that knife was their property since the knife described by John New was not located until 1899 [7]. Presenting the knife found by Holt may have convicted the suspects, since it would have given credence to the rest of New's testimony, but after nine years of expensive investigations and conflicting stories in the media most were ready to put the matter to rest.

Twelve

The Role of the Media and Politics

The cases of the William Gibson and John Frazer murders have proven that little has changed since 1890 in human nature and how people are persuaded to believe one thing or another. The confusion and conflict created by the media of the time reflects the atmosphere of the 21st century where everyone has an opinion and attempts to influence others to accept it. The only difference is the manner of transmission with the internet and social media spreading information globally.

It is interesting how with just printed media, rumors and legends can extend for decades, even centuries. Many of the newspapers simply printed what another published and some published different facts than others. Few seem to have all the facts presented at once or the same facts.

Politics should never enter a criminal investigation, however, even today that situation has not changed, especially regarding cover-ups. When the public or officials decide what occurred during a crime often relevant evidence is hidden because it does not reflect the predominate theory or facts not relevant or proven dominate the investigation.

The article published in the Kansas City Star in August of 1892 did much to formulate the stories that would filter down for generations in Elk and Chautauqua Counties. The rumors went from nine people murdering Frazer to 40 or 50 being involved. One story that seemed to make sense was that there were nine men that all took a stab at Frazer so that all would be equally guilty. The author heard that version growing up. It is entirely possible, but more than likely the number of suspects increased due to the large reward money offered of $1000 a suspect.

The political climate also muddied the waters with Republicans and the Populists parties at constant odds over the railroads at the center of disputes. The Farmer's Alliance was assumed to have been behind the murder of Frazer, and possibly his partner, William Gibson, without any proof at all. The elusive group, The Livestock Protection Association, might have actually existed with the acquitted suspects being members or even Wesley Best. This bit of information came from the two amateur detectives Davis and West, so the validity is questionable since profit was their primary motive.

The outcome of the trials might have been very different if the murder weapon had been discovered during the investigations and trials. The weight of the cases against the Coxes, Leckliter and Burgess lay squarely on the testimony of John New and when the first knife was found to not match the description he gave of the murder weapon produced by Cox, the test of his story lost credence. Very unfortunate as most likely he was telling the truth.

The fate of the physical evidence is unknown, but might produce some interesting results today with advances in forensics. The bloody clothes and knife discovered in 1899 could answer 130 year old questions about the identity of the killers. What would not be addressed is why such savagery against Frazer and not Gibson? The poisoning of Gibson in Moline seemed to be just "taking care of business" and removing him from the economic scene in Elk County, but what warranted the butchery of John Frazer?

Since the legal documents from 1894 are lost the question remains on what basis did the law decide not to continue investigating Wesley Best. John New made it clear it was Best who paid the conspirators to murder John S. Frazer, so why he was not charged in 1896?

Frazer and Gibson both bought up land at sheriff auctions, so why did Frazer warrant the death he received? Gibson primarily dealt in short horn cattle when he joined force with Frazer and his Longhorns, but the decision was his to deal in Texas cattle. While Gibson was known to display a temper when provoked, nothing is ever mentioned about Frazer except flattery.

The estates for Gibson and Frazer were still in probate in 1893 with debts owed to those losing money to losses from Tick Fever in addition to bank loans. Since Frazer was making the rounds to farmers writing checks for dead cattle one wonders what purpose killing him served before the checks were written and cashed. Probate cases can drag on for years with only pennies on the dollar being recovered, so why was murder the solution? There must have been some other underlying issue that is not apparent and may yet come to light.

The murderers of William H. Gibson and John S. Frazer never paid for the crime and the deeds remain officially unsolved. The men charged in 1894 and tried in 1896 were probably the perpetrators along with Franklin Olney, Wesley Best and perhaps others.

End Notes

Chapter One
History of Elk and Chautauqua Counties

1. Elk County Historical Society, "History of Elk County", accessed November 21, 2019, http://www.kancoll.org/books/cutler/elk/elk-co-p5.html
2. Ibid
3. Editor of The Daily World, C.S. Burch Publishing Co., Chicago 1886. Handbook of Elk and Chautauqua Counties.

Chapter Two
Kansas, the Cattle Industry and Tick Fever

1. Handbook of Texas Online, Tamara Miner Haygood, "TEXAS FEVER," accessed November 21, 2019.
2. Ibid
3. 1851 – 1917, Cattle Drives and Texas Fever, Brian Altonen, MPH, MS, accessed November 21, 2019,
4. Jimmy M. Skaggs, The Cattle-Trailing Industry: Between Supply and Demand, 1866–1890, page 114
5. Ibid page 107
6. "It is Here! Splenic or Spanish Fever", The Moline Mercury (Moline, Kansas) June 27, 1890 Retrieved June 16, 2019
7. "Crime Most Foul", The Moline Republican (Moline, Kansas) July 4, 1890)

Chapter Three

The Murder of William Harrison Gibson

1. "William H. Gibson Dead", The Howard Courant (Howard, Kansas) May 30, 1890. Retrieved June 17, 2019.
2. (The Buffalo Morning Express and Illustrated Buffalo Express (Buffalo, New York) September 9, 1892)
3. The Sedan Graphic (Sedan, Kansas) May 28, 1890, page 3. Retrieved August 6, 2020.
4. Paradise Messenger (Paradise, Texas) August 2, 1890. Retrieved September 7, 2020

Chapter Four
The Murder and Inquest of John Samuel Frazer

1. "Murder! John S. Frazer the Victim!" The Weekly Times Star (Sedan, Kansas) July 4, 1890 Retrieved June 15, 2020
2. Ibid.
3. Ibid.
4. "A Horrible Crime: John S. Frazer Murdered", Cedar Vale Commercial (Cedar Vale, Kansas) Page 4 Sat, Jul 5, 1890 · Page 4 Downloaded on Sep 21, 2019
5. Ibid.
6. Ibid.
7. "Murder Will Out", The Coffeyville Weekly Journal (Coffeyville, Kansas) Friday, Aug 24, 1894, page 1. Retrieved on Sep 21, 2019,
8. "It is Here! Splenic or Spanish Fever", The Moline Mercury (Moline, Kansas) June 27, 1890 Retrieved June 16, 2019

Chapter Five
The Investigation Begins in Chautauqua County 1890

1. "The Frazer Murder", The Longton Gleaner (Longton, Kansas) Fri, Jul 11, 1890. Page 3 Retrieved on Sep 21, 2019.
2. "Murder: John S. Frazer the Victim", The Sedan Graphic (Sedan, Kansas) Wed., Jul 2, 1890. Page 3 Retrieved on Sep 21, 2019.
3. "Not Captured!" The Moline Republican (Moline, Kansas) July 11, 1890. Retrieved on Sep 21, 2019.
4. Ibid.
5. Ibid.
6. Ibid.
7. "Frank Davis arrested." The Moline Republican (Moline, Kansas) Friday, Jul 25, 1890. Page 4 Retrieved on Sep 21, 2019.

Chapter Six
The Elk and Chautauqua County Investigations 1890 -1893

1. "Frank Davis arrested." The Moline Republican (Moline, Kansas) Friday, Jul 25, 1890. Page 4 Retrieved on Sep 21, 2019.
2. Ibid.
3. "Arrested for the Frazer Murder", The Cedar Vale Star (Cedar Vale, Kansas) Friday, Sep 2, 1892, page 2 Retrieved on Sep 21, 2019.
4. "Resolutions", The Elk County Citizen (Howard, Kansas) July 9, 1890, page 3. Retrieved on Sep 21, 2019.
5. "The State vs Hutton and Kimsey", The Coffeyville Weekly Journal (Coffeyville, Kansas) Friday, Sept. 16, 1892, page 2. Retrieved on Sept 21, 2019,
6. Ibid.

7. "Queer Tactics: Dragging Crime Into Politics", Kansas City Times (KC Missouri) September 1, 1892. Retrieved June 25, 2020
8. "Humphrey's Humbug", The Advocate (Topeka, Kansas) Wed, Sept. 7, 1892, page 1. Retrieved on Sep 21, 2019
9. "A Political Crime: What Use the Republican Party Made of the Frazer Murder", Pittsburgh Kansan September 22, 1892. Retrieved March 27, 2020.

Chapter Seven
More Arrests in 1894

1. "Brought to Bay", The Daily World (Girard, Kansas) Thursday, Aug 23, 1894, page 1.
2. Ibid.
3. "For the Murder of Frazer", The Citizen (Howard, Kansas) August 23, 1894. Retrieved Sept. 1, 2019.
4. Kansas City Times (KC Missouri) August 23, 1894. Retrieved June 25, 2020.
5. Ibid.
6. "Still Talking", The Weekly Times Star (Sedan, Kansas) September 21, 1894.
7. Ibid.
8. Ibid.
9. The Moline Republican (Moline, Kansas) Sept 28, 1894, page 2.
10. Ibid.
11. "Only One Incident", The Moline Republican (Moline, Kansas) May 15, 1896. Page 2.
12. "Dismissed", The Howard Courant (Howard, Kansas) Friday, Sep 7, 1894, page 3. Retrieved on Sept 21, 2019.

Chapter Eight
Preliminary Hearing
March 16, 1896 at Sedan, Chautauqua County

1. "The Frazer Murder", The Weekly Star and Kansas (Independence, Kansas) March 20, 1896. Retrieved April 16, 2020.
2. Ibid.
3. "New Tells a Blood Curdling Story", The Weekly Times Star (Sedan, Kansas) March 20, 1896, page 3.
4. Ibid.
5. Ibid.
6. Ibid.

Chapter Nine
The Testimony of John F. New
March 17, 1896 Chautauqua County. Kansas

1. "New Tells a Blood Curdling Story", The Weekly Times Star (Sedan, Kansas) March 20, 1896, page 3.
2. Ibid.
3. Ibid.
4. "The Frazer Murder Again" Wilson County Citizen (Fredonia, Kansas) September 1, 1899. Page 2.
5. "New Tells a Blood Curdling Story", The Weekly Times Star (Sedan, Kansas) March 20, 1896, page 3.

Chapter Ten
Further Testimony on March 18, 1896 Chautauqua County, Kansas

1. "New Tells a Blood Curdling Story", The Weekly Times Star (Sedan, Kansas) March 20, 1896, page 2.
2. Ibid.
3. Ibid.
4. Ibid.

Chapter Eleven
The Trials Begin 1895 and 1896

1. "A Puzzling Crime", The Kansas Semi-Weekly Capitol (Topeka, Kansas) Nov 24, 1896.
2. The Weekly Times Star (Sedan, Kansas) September 4, 1896.
3. Ibid.
4. Ibid.
5. Ibid.
6. Ibid.
7. Wilson County Citizen (Fredonia, Kansas) September 1, 1899. Page 2, "The Frazer Murder Again".

Bibliography

Books

J. Evetts Haley, "Texas Fever and the Winchester Quarantine," Panhandle-Plains Historical Review 8 (1935).

Miodrag Ristic and Julius P. Kreier, Babesiosis (New York: Academic, 1981).

Jimmy M. Skaggs, The Cattle-Trailing Industry: Between Supply and Demand, 1866–1890 (Lawrence: University Press of Kansas, 1973).

Editor of The Daily World, C.S. Burch Publishing Co., Chicago 1886. Handbook of Elk and Chautauqua Counties.
https://www.kansasmemory.org/item/225066/page/1

Web Pages

Handbook of Texas Online, Tamara Miner Haygood, "TEXAS FEVER," accessed November 21, 2019, http://www.tshaonline.org/handbook/online/articles/awt01.

Elk County Historical Society, "History of Elk County", accessed November 21, 2019,
http://www.kancoll.org/books/cutler/elk/elk-co-p5.html

1851 – 1917, Cattle Drives and Texas Fever, Brian Altonen, MPH, MS, accessed November 21, 2019,
https://brianaltonenmph.com/gis/historical-disease-maps/zoonoses/1866-1885-the-texas-cattle-drives-and-texas-fever/

Kansas Conflict: Populist Versus Railroader in the 1890s, Donald E. Press Autumn 1977 (Vol. 43, No. 3), pages 319 to 333
Transcribed by Tod Roberts; digitized with permission of the Kansas Historical Society.
https://www.kshs.org/index.php?url=p/kansas-historical-quarterly-kansas-conflict-populist-versus-railroader-in-the-1890s/13274   Retrieved March 26, 2020

Land Rush of 1889 - Wikipedia

The Oklahoma Land Run of 1889 was the first land run into the Unassigned Lands. The area that was opened to settlement included all or part of the Canadian, Cleveland, Kingfisher, Logan, Oklahoma, and Payne counties of the US state of Oklahoma.[1] The land run started at high noon on April 22, 1889, with an estimated 50,000 people lined up for their piece of the available two million acres (8,000 km^2).[2]

Boomers and Sooners: The Oklahoma Land Rush of 1889, Jenny Ashcraft

Boomers and Sooners: The Oklahoma Land Rush of 1889 - Fishwrap The official blog of Newspapers.com

"When the clock struck 12:00 on the 22nd, the mad rush began. Those who snuck into the territory early concealed themselves in ravines and bushes, and when the bugle sounded "seemed to rise right up out of the ground" to claim the property. Thousands poured into Guthrie, Oklahoma, which saw it's population go from 10 in the morning to 15,000 by nightfall. Oklahoma City experienced similar growth and there were more than 11,000 filings for homestead land by the end of the day. Bitter resentment arose towards Sooners who entered the territory early. This led to many court cases for years to come where litigants protested hundreds of claims. The loss of tribal lands further marginalized Native Americans who saw additional land rushes take more tribal lands in subsequent years.

In 1890, the Unassigned Lands became the Oklahoma Territory and in 1907, Oklahoma became the 46th state. To learn more about the Oklahoma Land Rush."

Boomers and Sooners: The Oklahoma Land Rush of 1889 - Fishwrap The official blog of Newspapers.com

Maps

Outline map of Elk County, Kansas. Retrieved May 21, 2020

https://www.kansasmemory.org/item/223994/page/4

Chautauqua County Kansas 1887

Kansas Historical Society, Retrieved June 1, 2020

Elk and Chautauqua County platt maps from 1885 to1900

Newspapers

1885 to 1889

Railroad time tables, various ads, The Moline Mercury (Moline, Kansas) March 4, 1887. Retrieved April 19, 2020

https://www.newspapers.com/browse/us/kansas/moline/the-moline-republican_7418

"Frazer's New Addition to the City of Moline", The Moline Mercury (Moline, Kansas) March 11, 1887. Retrieved April 19, 2020

https://www.newspapers.com/browse/us/kansas/moline/the-moline-republican_7418

"Steve Frazer", The Moline Free Press (Moline, Kansas) March 13, 1885. Retrieved on November 10, 2020

https://www.newspapers.com/browse/us/kansas/moline/the-moline-republican_7418

"In and About Town", The Moline Mercury (Moline, Kansas) March 29, 1889 Retrieved June 16, 2020

https://www.newspapers.com/browse/us/kansas/moline/the-moline-republican_7418

"Mr. T.S. Frazer", The Moline Mercury (Moline, Kansas) April 1, 1887. Retrieved April 19, 2020

https://www.newspapers.com/browse/us/kansas/moline/the-moline-republican_7418

"Page one-various ads", The Moline Mercury (Moline, Kansas) May 8, 1885. Retrieved June 15, 2020

https://www.newspapers.com/browse/us/kansas/moline/the-moline-republican_7418

"Moline Stock Sales", The Moline Mercury (Moline, Kansas) May 31, 1889. Retrieved June 16, 2020

https://www.newspapers.com/browse/us/kansas/moline/the-moline-republican_7418

Various ads, The Moline Mercury (Moline, Kansas) June 8, 1888. Retrieved April 19, 2020

https://www.newspapers.com/browse/us/kansas/moline/the-moline-republican_7418

"John Frazer went to Kansas City", The Moline Mercury (Moline, Kansas) June 22, 1888,

Retrieved April 19, 2020

https://www.newspapers.com/browse/us/kansas/moline/the-moline-republican_7418

Various ads and announcements", The Moline Mercury (Moline, Kansas) July 3, 1885.

Retrieved April 19, 2020

https://www.newspapers.com/browse/us/kansas/moline/the-moline-republican_7418

"The Case of Myers vs Frazer", The Moline Mercury (Moline, Kansas) December 9, 1887 Retrieved June 16, 2010

https://www.newspapers.com/browse/us/kansas/moline/the-moline-republican_7418

Various announcements, The Moline Republican (Moline, Kansas) April 18, 1890. Retrieved June 16, 2020

https://www.newspapers.com/browse/us/kansas/moline/the-moline-republican_7418

The Sedan Graphic (Sedan, Kansas) May 28, 1890, page 3. Retrieved August 6, 2020.

https://www.newspapers.com/browse/us/kansas/sedan/the-sedan-graphic_6872

"William H. Gibson Dead", The Howard Courant (Howard, Kansas) May 30, 1890. Retrieved June 17, 2019

30 May 1890, 3 - The Howard Courant at Newspapers.com

"It's Here! Splenic Fever", The Moline Republican (Moline, Kansas) June 27, 1890 Retrieved June 16, 2019

https://www.newspapers.com/browse/us/kansas/moline/the-moline-republican_7418

General advertisements and background material. The Howard Courant (Howard, Kansas) August 1, 1890. Retrieved June 29, 2020

https://www.newspapers.com/browse/us/kansas/howard/the-howard-courant_8079

"Losses Avenged", Kansas City Times (KC Missouri) July 1, 1890. Retrieved June 25, 2020

https://www.newspapers.com/browse/us/missouri/kansas-city/the-kansas-city-times_1891

"Murder: John S. Frazer the Victim", The Sedan Graphic (Sedan, Kansas) Wed., Jul 2, 1890. Page 3 Retrieved on Sep 21, 2019,

https://kansashistoricalsociety.newspapers.com/image/366740608

"Murder: John S. Frazer the Victim", The Elk City Enterprise (Elk City, Kansas) Thursday, Jul 3, 1890 Page 1 Retrieved on Sep 21, 2019,

https://kansashistoricalsociety.newspapers.com/image/367238729

"Murder! John S. Frazer the Victim!", The Weekly Times Star (Sedan, Kansas) July 4, 1890. Retrieved June 15, 2020

https://www.newspapers.com/browse/us/kansas/independence/the-weekly-star-and-kansan_3928

"Crime Most Foul", The Moline Republican (Moline, Kansas) Friday, July 4, 1890. Page 1 Retrieved on Sep 21, 2019,

https://kansashistoricalsociety.newspapers.com/image/383542513

"A Horrible Crime: John S. Frazer Murdered", Cedar Vale Commercial (Cedar Vale, Kansas) Page 4 Sat, Jul 5, 1890, page 4. Retrieved on Sep 21, 2019.

https://kansashistoricalsociety.newspapers.com/image/366728887

"Resolutions", The Elk County Citizen (Howard, Kansas) July 9, 1890, page 3. Retrieved on Sep 21, 2019.
https://www.newspapers.com/browse/us/kansas/howard/the-citizen_8078

"The Frazer Murder", The Longton Gleaner (Longton, Kansas) Fri, Jul 11, 1890. Page 3 Retrieved on Sep 21, 2019,
https://kansashistoricalsociety.newspapers.com/image/489709428

"Funeral Notice", The Moline Republican (Moline, Kansas) Friday, Jul 11, 1890, page 4. Retrieved on Sep 21, 2019,
https://kansashistoricalsociety.newspapers.com/image/383542525

"Not Captured!" The Moline Republican (Moline, Kansas) July 11, 1890. Retrieved on Sep 21, 2019.
https://www.newspapers.com/browse/us/kansas/moline/the-moline-republican_7418

"The Murder: The Inquest a Flat Failure", The Sedan Times Journal (Sedan, Kansas) July 11, 1890. Retrieved June 29, 2020
https://www.newspapers.com/browse/us/kansas/sedan/the-weekly-times-star_6726

"Frank Davis arrested." The Moline Republican (Moline, Kansas) Friday, Jul 25, 1890. Page 4 Retrieved on Sep 21, 2019,
https://kansashistoricalsociety.newspapers.com/image/383542542

"John S. Frazer", The Weekly Times-Star (Sedan, Kansas) Friday, Jul 25, 1890. Page 3 Retrieved on Sep 21, 2019,
https://kansashistoricalsociety.newspapers.com/image/367562691

"The Sedan Graphic (Sedan, Kansas) July 23, 1890, page 3. Retrieved August 6, 2020.
https://www.newspapers.com/browse/us/kansas/sedan/the-sedan-graphic_6872

"Not Captured!", The Moline Republican (Moline, Kansas) July 11, 1890. Retrieved on August 21, 2020
https://www.newspapers.com/browse/us/kansas/moline/the-moline-republican_7418

"Notice of Appointment, Administrator", The Moline Republican (Moline, Kansas) Friday, Aug 22, 1890. Page 4 Retrieved on Sep 21, 2019,
https://kansashistoricalsociety.newspapers.com/image/383542619

"Impending Conflict", Paradise Messenger (Paradise, Texas) August 2, 1890, page 6. Retrieved September 7, 2020
https://www.newspapers.com/browse/us/texas/paradise/paradise-messenger_1319

"Murder!" The Sedan Times-Journal (Sedan, Kansas) July 4, 1890, page 3. Retrieved on November 10, 2020

https://www.newspapers.com/browse/us/kansas/sedan/the-weekly-times-star_6726

1891

Howard State Bank ad, Moline Republican (Moline, Kansas) February 20, 1891. Retrieved April 19, 2020

https://www.newspapers.com/browse/us/kansas/moline/the-moline-republican_7418

"The Cattle Suits", The Moline Republican (Moline, Kansas) June 19, 1891. Retrieved April 18, 2020

https://www.newspapers.com/browse/us/kansas/moline/the-moline-republican_7418

"Administrator's Sale", The Moline Republican, Aug 1, 1891. Retrieved March 29, 2020

https://www.newspapers.com/browse/us/kansas/moline/the-moline-republican_7418

"The Gallion-Crawford Letter", The Moline Republican (Moline, Kansas) November 13, 1891. Retrieved June 7, 2020

https://www.newspapers.com/image/383543930/?terms=John%2BS.%2BFrazer%2C%2BKansas

1892

"Publications Notice", Sedan Republic January 27, 1892. Retrieved March 27, 2020

https://www.newspapers.com/image/366799577

"Publication Notice Frazer Estate" Sedan Republican (Sedan, Kansas) Wed., Jan 27, 1892, Page 2

Retrieved on Sep 21, 2019

https://kansashistoricalsociety.newspapers.com/image/366799577

"Notice of Final Settlement", The Moline Republican (Moline, Kansas) Friday, Feb 19, 1892. Page 4 Retrieved on Sep 21, 2019,

https://kansashistoricalsociety.newspapers.com/image/383544265

"Turn On the Light: The Murderers of John S. Frazer Escape Justice", The Freeman's Lance (Sedan, Kansas) Friday, Apr 8, 1892. Page 4 Retrieved on Sep 21, 2019,

https://kansashistoricalsociety.newspapers.com/image/366804934

"A Rotten Party", The Weekly Star and Kansan (Independence, Kansas) April 15, 1892, page 2. Retrieved August 27, 2020 https://www.newspapers.com/browse/us/kansas/independence/the-weekly-star-and-kansan_3928

"Free Criminals: More about the Murders of John S. Frazer", The Elk County Citizen (Howard, Kansas) Wed., May 11, 1892, page 1. Retrieved on Sep 21, 2019,
https://kansashistoricalsociety.newspapers.com/image/419745964

"Queer Tactics: Dragging Crime Into Politics", Kansas City Times (KC Missouri) September 1, 1892. Retrieved June 25, 2020
https://www.newspapers.com/browse/us/missouri/kansas-city/the-kansas-city-times_1891

The Kansas City Times (Kansas City Missouri) September 11, 1892. Retrieved August 27, 2020
https://www.newspapers.com/browse/us/missouri/kansas-city/the-kansas-city-times_1891

"Arrested for the Frazer Murder", The Cedar Vale Star (Cedar Vale, Kansas) Friday, Sep 2, 1892, page 2 Retrieved on Sep 21, 2019
https://kansashistoricalsociety.newspapers.com/image/419602379

"Humphrey's Humbug", The Advocate (Topeka, Kansas) Wed, Sept. 7, 1892, page 1. Retrieved on Sept. 21, 2019
https://kansashistoricalsociety.newspapers.com/image/70818118

"Charged With Murder", The Roanoke Times (Roanoke, Virginia) September 2, 1892, page 4. Retrieved September 7, 2020
https://www.newspapers.com/browse/us/virginia/roanoke/the-roanoke-times_1742

"The Trial: A Weak Case Against Hutton and Kimsey", The Cedar Vale Star (Cedar Vale, Kansas) Friday, Sep 9, 1892, page 2. Retrieved on Sep 21, 2019,
https://kansashistoricalsociety.newspapers.com/image/419602502

"Response to Kansas City Journal", Harper Advocate (Harper, Kansas) September 9, 1892. Retrieved April 11, 2020
https://www.newspapers.com/browse/us/kansas/harper/harper-advocate_8070

"The Kansas Murder" The Buffalo Morning Express and Illustrated Buffalo Express (Buffalo, New York) Front page. September 9, 1892. Retrieved August 6, 2020
https://www.newspapers.com/browse/us/new-york/buffalo/buffalo-morning-express-and-illustrated-buffalo-express_6147.

"The State vs Hutton and Kimsey", The Coffeyville Weekly Journal (Coffeyville, Kansas) Friday, Sept. 16, 1892, page 2. Retrieved on Sept 21, 2019,
https://kansashistoricalsociety.newspapers.com/image/56924967

"The Sedan Investigation", The Girard Press (Girard, Kansas) Thursday, Sep 15, page 4. Retrieved on Sep 21, 2019,
https://kansashistoricalsociety.newspapers.com/image/186531473

"A Chautauqua Man's Statement', The Industrial Free Press (Winfield, Kansas) Thursday, Sep 15, 1892, page 8. Retrieved on Sep 21, 2019,
https://kansashistoricalsociety.newspapers.com/image/489344161

"A Political Crime: What Use the Republican Party Made of the Frazer Murder", Pittsburgh Kansan September 22, 1892. Retrieved March 27, 2020
https://www.newspapers.com/image/483310603/

1894

"Brought to Bay", The Daily World (Girard, Kansas) Thursday, Aug 23, 1894, page 1. Retrieved on Sept. 21, 2019
https://kansashistoricalsociety.newspapers.com/image/368636035

"Charged With Murder", Kansas City Times (KC Missouri) August 23, 1894. Retrieved June 25, 2020
https://www.newspapers.com/browse/us/missouri/kansas-city/the-kansas-city-times_1891

"For the Murder of Frazer", The Citizen (Howard, Kansas) August 23, 1894. Retrieved Sept. 1, 2019.
https://www.newspapers.com/browse/us/kansas/howard/the-citizen_8078

"Murder Will Out", The Coffeyville Weekly Journal (Coffeyville, Kansas) Friday, Aug 24, 1894, page 4. Retrieved on Sep 21, 2019,
https://kansashistoricalsociety.newspapers.com/image/58991116

"Brought to Bay: Five Men Arrested for the Murder of John S. Frazer", The Grenola Greeting and Chief (Grenola, Kansas) Friday, Aug 24, 1894, page 1. Retrieved on Sep 21, 2019,
https://kansashistoricalsociety.newspapers.com/image/481413893

"Murder Will Out", The Weekly Star and Kansan (Independence, Kansas) Friday, Aug 24, 1894, page 2. .\Retrieved on Sep 21, 2019,
https://kansashistoricalsociety.newspapers.com/image/118309649

"The Frazer Murder", The Weekly Times-Star (Sedan, Kansas) Friday, Aug 24, 1894, page 3. Retrieved on Sep 21, 2019.
https://kansashistoricalsociety.newspapers.com/image/389100717

"An Old Murder Revived". The Farmers' Advocate (Winfield, Kansas) Aug 25, 1894, page 3. Retrieved on Sep 21, 2019,
https://kansashistoricalsociety.newspapers.com/image/489350627

"Arrested", The Freeman's Lance (Sedan, Kansas) Wednesday, Aug 29, 1894, page 2. Retrieved on Sept 21, 2019,
https://kansashistoricalsociety.newspapers.com/image/366750745

"A Doubtful Confession" Sedalia Democrat (Sedalia, Missouri) August 29, 1894. Retrieved December 31, 2020
https://www.newspapers.com/browse/us/missouri/sedalia/the-sedalia-democrat_653

"Sensational Arrests", Florence Bulletin (Florence, Kansas) Friday, Aug 31, 1894, page 3. Retrieved on Sep 21, 2019,
https://kansashistoricalsociety.newspapers.com/image/426074219

"Sensational Arrests", The National Field (Salina, Kansas) Friday, Aug 31, 1894, page 3. Retrieved on Sep 21, 2019,
https://kansashistoricalsociety.newspapers.com/image/485207899

"Gibson and Frazer's Murders", The Winchester Star (Winchester, Kansas) Friday, Aug 31, 1894, page 1. Retrieved on Sep 21, 2019,
https://kansashistoricalsociety.newspapers.com/image/274241158

"The Evidence Relied On", The Western Star (Coldwater) Sept 1, 1894, page 2. Retrieved April 8, 2020 https://www.newspapers.com/browse/us/kansas/coldwater/the-western-star_7036

"Frazer Suspects Released", Weekly World (Pittsburgh, Kansas) September 6, 1894, page 7. Retrieved April 11, 2020
https://www.newspapers.com/browse/us/kansas/pittsburg/the-weekly-world_10793

"Dismissed", The Howard Courant (Howard, Kansas) Friday, Sep 7, 1894, page 3. Retrieved on Sept 21, 2019,
https://kansashistoricalsociety.newspapers.com/image/420245725

"A Fizzle", The Weekly Times Star (Sedan, Kansas) September 21, 1894. Retrieved January 2, 2021.
https://www.newspapers.com/browse/us/kansas/sedan/the-weekly-times-star_6726

"Still Talking", The Weekly Times Star (Sedan, Kansas) September 21, 1894. Retrieved April 16, 1894
https://www.newspapers.com/browse/us/kansas/sedan/the-weekly-times-star_6726

"Letter to Editor", The Moline Republican (Moline, Kansas) Sept 28, 1894. Retrieved April 9, 2020
https://www.newspapers.com/browse/us/kansas/moline/the-moline-republican_7418

The Moline Republican (Moline, Kansas) Sept 28, 1894, page 2. Retrieved December 28, 2020.
https://www.newspapers.com/browse/us/kansas/moline/the-moline-republican_7418

"Kansas News Items-William Leckliter", The Narka News (Narka, Kansas) September 28, 1894. Retrieved April 16, 2020

https://www.newspapers.com/browse/us/kansas/narka/the-narka-news_7073

"From Mr. Cox", The Moline Republican (Moline, Kansas) October 5, 1894. Retrieved April 11, 2020

https://www.newspapers.com/browse/us/kansas/moline/the-moline-republican_7418

1896

"Frazer Murderers", The Topeka Daily Capitol, March 19, 1896. Retrieved Nov. 18, 2019.

https://www.newspapers.com/browse/us/kansas/topeka/the-topeka-daily-capital_2577

"The Frazer Murder", The Weekly Star and Kansas (Independence, Kansas) March 20, 1896, page 4. Retrieved April 16, 2020

https://www.newspapers.com/browse/us/kansas/independence/the-weekly-star-and-kansan_3928

"New Tells a Blood Curdling Story", The Weekly Times Star (Sedan, Kansas) March 20, 1896 Retrieved April 19, 2020

https://www.newspapers.com/browse/us/kansas/sedan/the-weekly-times-star_6726

"Keenen Hurst's, Adventure" Independence Daily Reporter (Independence, Kansas) May 12, 1896 Retrieved April 16, 1896

https://www.newspapers.com/browse/us/kansas/independence/independence-daily-reporter_3595

"Only One Incident", The Moline Republican (Moline, Kansas) May 15, 1896. Page 2 Retrieved April 11, 2020.

https://www.newspapers.com/browse/us/kansas/moline/the-moline-republican_7418

The Weekly Times Star (Sedan, Kansas) September 4, 1896. Retrieved May 13, 2020.

https://www.newspapers.com/browse/us/kansas/sedan/the-weekly-times-star_6726

"District Court Doings", Democratic Messenger (Eureka, Kansas) Nov 13, 1896. Retrieved April 9, 2020.

https://www.newspapers.com/browse/us/kansas/eureka/democratic-messenger_7279

"Famous Case Ended", The Evening Herald (Ottawa, Kansas) November 20, 1896. Retrieved April 11, 2020.

https://www.newspapers.com/browse/us/kansas/ottawa/the-evening-herald_3348

"Famous Case Ended. Accused Murderers of John S. Frazer Acquitted", The Kansas Semi-Weekly Capital (Topeka) November 20, 1896. Retrieved May 26, 2020.

https://www.newspapers.com/browse/us/missouri/kansas-city/kansas-city-journal_1553

"Ends in Acquittal", The Leavenworth Times November 20, 1896. Retrieved May 26, 2020

https://www.newspapers.com/browse/us/kansas/leavenworth/the-leavenworth-times_621

"Famous Case Ended", Independence Daily Reporter (Independence, Kansas) Sat, Nov 21, 1896, page 4. Retrieved on Sep 21, 2019

https://kansashistoricalsociety.newspapers.com/image/95958053

"A Puzzling Crime", The Kansas Semi-Weekly Capitol (Topeka, Kansas) Nov 24, 1896. Retrieved April 13, 2020

https://www.newspapers.com/browse/us/kansas/topeka/the-kansas-semi-weekly-capital_7499

"A Puzzling Crime", The Kansas Semi-Weekly Capital (Topeka) November 24, 1896. Retrieved May 26, 2020

https://www.newspapers.com/browse/us/kansas/topeka/the-kansas-semi-weekly-capital_7499

1897

"John New is out of jail", The Moline Republican (Moline, Kansas) January 8, 1897. Retrieved May 26, 2020.

https://www.newspapers.com/browse/us/kansas/moline/the-moline-republican_7418

"John New, et al, Again", The Weekly Times-Star (Sedan, Kansas) Friday July 30, 1897, page 3. Retrieved on Sep 21, 2019.

https://kansashistoricalsociety.newspapers.com/image/367543509

Ad for Wesley Best mill, Modern Light (Columbus, Kansas) December 9, 1897, page f4. Retrieved May 26, 2020

https://www.newspapers.com/browse/us/kansas/columbus/modern-light_8265

"Oley and Company ad, The Howard Courant (Howard, Kansas) December 17, 1897, page 2. Retrieved May 26, 2020.

https://www.newspapers.com/browse/us/kansas/howard/the-howard-courant_8079

1899

"The Frazer Murder Again", Wilson County Citizen (Fredonia, Kansas) September 1, 1899. Page 2, Retrieved August 6, 2020.

https://www.newspapers.com/browse/us/kansas/fredonia/wilson-county-citizen_8155

1900

"Potpourri" The Howard Courant (Howard, Kansas) June 8, 1900. Retrieved May 26, 2020

https://www.newspapers.com/browse/us/kansas/howard/the-howard-courant_8079

Appendix

Court Documents 1890 to 1896 for Chautauqua and Greenwood Counties Kansas

State of Kansas, Chautauqua County, Warrant March 6, 1896. Kansas Historical Society. Arrest warrant for Burgess, McBee, Cox and New. Warrant issued from Justice of the Peace Ellis. Retrieved June 30, 2020.

State of Kansas, Chautauqua County, Criminal Action No. 199 March 6, 1896. Kansas Historical Society. Murder charges for James Burgess, Theo Cox, William Leckliter, Mark McBee and John New. County Attorney McBrian. Retrieved June 30, 2020. Describes various alias warrants issued from March 6 to 14.

State of Kansas, Chautauqua County, Warrant March 7, 1896. Kansas Historical Society. Arrest warrant for Burgess, McBee, Cox and New. Sheriff warrant from Sheriff Taylor. Retrieved June 30, 2020.

State of Kansas, Chautauqua County, Subpoena, March 12, 1896. Kansas Historical Society. Kansas vs James Burgess and others. For defense, Mark McBee, Franklin S. Olney, J. Marshall, John Kiefson, Kate Kiefson, L. Flagler, T. Shafen and Walter A. McCausland. Filed by Justice of the Peace Ellis. Retrieved June 30, 2020.

State of Kansas, Chautauqua County, Order of Commitment No. 199, March 7, 1896. Kansas Historical Society. Kansas vs James Burgess and others. Sheriff Kiser. Retrieved June 30, 2020.

State of Kansas, Chautauqua County, Subpoena, March 13, 1896. Kansas Historical Society. Kansas vs James Burgess and others. Witnesses for the State, W.W. Litell and D.M. Woodsworth. Retrieved June 30, 2020.

State of Kansas, Chautauqua County, Subpoena, March 13, 1896. Kansas Historical Society. Kansas vs James Burgess and others. For John Cleveland, John W. Hansen and J.R. Glascock. Filed by Justice of the Peace Ellis. Retrieved June 30, 2020.

State of Kansas, Chautauqua County, Subpoena, March 13, 1896. Kansas Historical Society. Kansas vs James Burgess and others. For Mahala Arbridge,

John Glenn and Mahala Gibson. Filed by Justice of the Peace Ellis. Retrieved June 30, 2020.

State of Kansas, Chautauqua County, Amended Complaint, March 14, 1896. Kansas Historical Society. Kansas vs James Burgess and others. John F New added. County Attorney McBrian. Retrieved June 30, 2020.

State of Kansas, Chautauqua County, Warrant No. 199, March 14, 1896. Kansas Historical Society. Kansas vs James Burgess, Mark McBee, Theo Cox, William Leckliter and John New. Sheriff Kiser. Retrieved June 30, 2020.

State of Kansas, Chautauqua County, Arrest Warrant No. 199, March 14, 1896. Kansas Historical Society. For Mark McBee, Theo Cox, William Leckliter and John F. New from Justice of the Peace Ellis. Retrieved June 30, 2020.

State of Kansas, Chautauqua County, Complaint, Exhibit 2, March 14, 1896. Kansas Historical Society. Murder charges for James Burgess, Theo Cox, William Leckliter, Mark McBee and John New. From Justice of the Peace Ellis. List of witnesses and jury. Retrieved June 30, 2020.

State of Kansas, Chautauqua County, Subpoena, March 16, 1896. Kansas Historical Society. Kansas vs James Burgess and others. For Mahala Arbridge, Ben Kelley and Harriet Gibson. Filed by Justice of the Peace Ellis. Retrieved June 30, 2020.

State of Kansas, Chautauqua County, Subpoena No. 199, March 16, 1896. Kansas Historical Society. Kansas vs James Burgess and others. For Frank McCaslin and Dan Ellis. Filed by Justice of the Peace Ellis. Retrieved June 30, 2020.

State of Kansas, Chautauqua County, Subpoena 207, March 16, 1896. Kansas Historical Society, Witness subpoena for. Daniel M. Woodworth and William Littel from Justice of the Peace Ellis. Retrieved June 30, 2020.

State of Kansas, Chautauqua County, Warrant No. 199, March 16, 1896. Kansas Historical Society. Kansas vs James Burgess and other. Sheriff Kiser. Retrieved June 30, 2020.

State of Kansas, Chautauqua County, Subpoena no. 199, March 16, 1896. Kansas Historical Society. Kansas vs James Burgess and others. Sheriff Kiser. For Abe Harris. Retrieved June 30, 2020.

State of Kansas, Chautauqua County, Subpoena no. 199, March 16, 1896. Kansas Historical Society. Kansas vs James Burgess and others. Sheriff Kiser. For A.C. Kenneson, E.C. Mcbrian and H. R. Taylor. Served by Sheriff Harkats. Retrieved June 30, 2020.

State of Kansas, Chautauqua County, Subpoena, March 16, 1896. Kansas Historical Society. For defense, Susan H. Williams. Served by Sheriff Kiser. Filed by Justice of the Peace Ellis. Retrieved June 30, 2020.

State of Kansas, Chautauqua County, Arrest Warrant March 16, 1896. Kansas Historical Society. James Burgess, Theo Cox, William Leckliter, Mark McBee and John New. For Mark McBee. From Justice of the Peace Ellis. Retrieved June 30, 2020.

State of Kansas, Chautauqua County, Subpoena, March 17, 1896. Kansas Historical Society. Kansas vs James Burgess and others. For the Defense Florence Hamilton (McBride) and Mike Hanlon. Filed by Justice of the Peace Ellis. Retrieved June 30, 2020. (Handwritten-Florence at Cherryvale in restaurant. Mike at Caneyville, Kansas).

State of Kansas, Chautauqua County, Subpoena, March 17, 1896. Kansas Historical Society. Kansas vs James Burgess and others. For H.S. McCray and Ike Hudson and Clark Solomon Wicks. Served by Sheriff Kiser. Filed by Justice of the Peace Ellis. Retrieved June 30, 2020. [Fredonia handwritten top of page].

State of Kansas, Chautauqua County, Subpoena. Kansas vs James Burgess and others. Kansas Historical Society. March 17, 1896. Witnesses for Defense; Ellis, Lillie and Alice McGrew.

State of Kansas, Chautauqua County, Subpoena, March 18, 1896. Kansas Historical Society. Kansas vs James Burgess and others. Sheriff Kiser. For John M. Cooper, H.S. McCray and Ike Hudson. Served by County Attorney McBrian. Retrieved June 30, 2020.

State of Kansas, Chautauqua County, Subpoena, March 18, 1896. Kansas Historical Society. Kansas vs James Burgess and others. For defense, Susan H. Williams. Filed by Justice of the Peace Ellis. Retrieved June 30, 2020.

State of Kansas, Chautauqua County, Subpoena, March 18, 1896. Kansas Historical Society. Kansas vs James Burgess and others. For Bill Kimsey. Filed by Justice of the Peace Ellis. Retrieved June 30, 2020. (Charles and James Kimsey not found).

State of Kansas, Chautauqua County, Subpoena, March 18, 1896. Kansas Historical Society. Kansas vs James Burgess and others. For defense Bill, Charles and James Kimsey. Filed by Justice of the Peace Ellis. Retrieved June 30, 2020.

State of Kansas, Chautauqua County, Subpoena, March 18, 1896. Kansas Historical Society. Kansas vs James Burgess and others. For R.W. M. Roe, William Dory, James Fletcher and John Denton. Filed by Justice of the Peace Ellis. Retrieved June 30, 2020. (Handwritten-Mrs. Murphy Not found)

State of Kansas, Chautauqua County, Subpoena, March 18, 1896. Kansas Historical Society. Kansas vs James Burgess and others. For defense, Dr. James P. Graham. Filed by Justice of the Peace Ellis. Retrieved June 30, 2020.

State of Kansas, Chautauqua County, Subpoena No. 199, March 18, 1896. Kansas Historical Society. From Sheriff Kisser for Hiram McCray and J.T. [illegible]. Retrieved June 30, 2020.

State of Kansas, Chautauqua County, Complaint No. 199, March 18, 1896. Kansas Historical Society. Kansas vs James Burgess and others. Retrieved June 30, 2020.

State of Kansas, Chautauqua County, Subpoena, March 19, 1896. Kansas Historical Society. Kansas vs James Burgess and others. For defense, Susan H. Williams. Filed by Justice of the Peace Ellis. Retrieved June 30, 2020.

State of Kansas, Chautauqua County, Arrest warrant, March 20, 1896. Kansas Historical Society. For McBee, Theo Cox, William Leckliter from Justice of the Peace Ellis. Retrieved June 30, 2020.

State of Kansas, Chautauqua County, Subpoena, March 20, 1896. Kansas Historical Society, Witness subpoena for. Daniel M. Woodworth and William Little from Justice of the Peace Ellis. Retrieved June 30, 2020.

State of Kansas, Chautauqua County, Return to Writ of Habeas Corpus. Kansas vs James Burgess and others. Kansas Historical Society. Justice of the Peace Ellis and Sheriff Kaiser March 20, 1896. For Mark McBee, Theo Cox, William Leckliter, John F. New and James Burgess to be held over in Sedan jail.

State of Kansas, Chautauqua County, Subpoena no. 100, March 20, 1896. Kansas Historical Society. Kansas vs James Burgess and others. Sheriff Kiser. For John Barley, Alex Stewart, John Laflin, H.G. Hanah, Mark Haslen, Henry Brunell, G.F. Torel, A. Aldrige, (illegible), J.G. Birchfuld. Filed by Justice of the Peace Ellis. Witnesses not found. Retrieved June 30, 2020. [Howard handwritten top of page].

State of Kansas, Chautauqua County, Subpoena No. 199, March 26, 1896. Kansas Historical Society. Kansas vs James Burgess and others. For Plaintiff J.M. Harris. Filed by Justice of the Peace Ellis. Retrieved June 30, 2020. (John M. or Jane M. Harris)

State of Kansas, Chautauqua County, Transcript Criminal Action No. 199, March 28, 1896. Kansas Historical Society. Murder charges for James Burgess, Theo Cox, William Leckliter, Mark McBee and John New. From Justice of the Peace Ellis. Retrieved June 30, 2020.

State of Kansas, Chautauqua County, Transcript Journal Entry, March 28, 1896. Kansas Historical Society. Murder charges for James Burgess, Theo Cox, William Leckliter, Mark McBee and John New. From Justice of the Peace Ellis. List of witnesses and jury. Retrieved June 30, 2020.

State of Kansas, Chautauqua County, Writ of Habeas Corpus March 31, 1896. Kansas Historical Society. Murder charges for James Burgess, Theo Cox, William Leckliter, Mark McBee and John New. Before Judge Jackson in Sedan. Two pages. Bail set at $6000. Retrieved June 30, 2020.

State of Kansas, Chautauqua County, Writ of Habeas Corpus March 31, 1896. Kansas Historical Society. Habeas Corpus for James Burgess, Theo Cox, William Leckliter and Mark McBee for Defense witnesses; Christian Baker Leckliter, Charles Leckliter, Daniel Miles, Frank H. Keifer, Kate Keifer, John H. Cox, Walter A. Clausland, F. Schoffen, James J. Hamilton, William Crooks. Filed by Luther Scott. Retrieved June 30, 2020.

State of Kansas, Chautauqua County, Notice to Appear, 13th Judicial District. Kansas vs James Burgess and others. Kansas Historical Society. Judge Jackson March 31, 1896 at 2 pm at Sedan courthouse. For Mark McBee, Theo Cox, William Leckliter, John F. New and James Burgess.

State of Kansas, Chautauqua County, Application, June 2, 1896. Kansas Historical Society. Request for deposition of C.L. McKesson in Colorado Springs from defense attorneys for Burgess Nicholson and King. Retrieved June 30, 2020.

State of Kansas, Chautauqua County, Complaint, June 2, 1896. Kansas Historical Society. Murder charges for Burgess, Cox, Leckliter, McBee, New and Olney. From County Attorney McBrian. Retrieved June 30, 2020.

State of Kansas, Chautauqua County, Warrant for murder, June 4, 1896. Kansas Historical Society. Murder charges for Burgess, Cox, Leckliter, McBee, New and Olney. From Justice of the Peace Ellis. Retrieved June 30, 2020.

State of Kansas, Chautauqua County, Criminal Action, June 8, 1896. Kansas Historical Society. Murder charges for Burgess, Cox, Leckliter, McBee, New and Olney. From Justice of the Peace Ellis. Retrieved June 30, 2020.

State of Kansas, Chautauqua County, Bail bond, June 8, 1896. Kansas Historical Society. Bail bond for James Burgess and Franklin Olney. Retrieved June 30, 2020.

State of Kansas, Chautauqua County, Bail bond for first degree murder, June 8, 1896. Kansas Historical Society. Bail bond for James Burgess and Franklin Olney. Retrieved June 30, 2020.

State of Kansas, Chautauqua County, Bail bond for first degree murder, June 8, 1896. Kansas Historical Society. Bail bond for James Burgess and Franklin Olney. Retrieved June 30, 2020.

State of Kansas, Chautauqua County, Complaint, June 21, 1896. Kansas Historical Society. Murder charges against Dr. Franklin Olney. Justice of the Peace Ellis. Retrieved June 30, 2020.

State of Kansas, Chautauqua County, Notice, July 7, 1896. Kansas Historical Society. Request for deposition of Wesley Best in Nashville from defense attorneys for Burgess Nicholson and King. Retrieved June 30, 2020.

State of Kansas, Chautauqua County, Notice, July 9, 1896. Kansas Historical Society. Request for deposition of C. L. McKesson in Colorado Springs from County Attorney McBrian and defense attorneys for Burgess Nicholson and King. Retrieved June 30, 2020.

State of Kansas, Chautauqua County, Subpoena, July 17, 1896. Kansas Historical Society, Witness subpoena for William Jones, Silas Walker, Frank Burgess, Mary Burgess, Henry Turner, et al. Retrieved June 30, 2020.

State of Kansas, Chautauqua County, Application, August 13, 1896. Kansas Historical Society. Kansas vs James Burgess and others. To District Court of Chautauqua County. Defense request for deposition of, telegraph operator at the Santa Fe depot at Lansing and (illegible) in Leavenworth County. Retrieved June 30, 2020.

State of Kansas, Chautauqua County, Application, August 14, 1896. Kansas Historical Society. Kansas vs James Burgess and others. To District Court of Chautauqua County. Defense request for deposition of, U. Herron and Harvey Rhoads in the Oklahoma Territory. Retrieved June 30, 2020.

State of Kansas, Chautauqua County, Kansas Historical Society. Kansas vs James Burgess and others. Deposition of telegraph operator from Lansing, W. G. Wells. August 15, 1896. Retrieved June 30, 2020.

State of Kansas, Chautauqua County, Application, August 22, 1896. Kansas Historical Society. Kansas vs James Burgess and others. To District Court of Chautauqua County. Defense request for deposition of, S. Whitlock in Howard, Kansas. Retrieved June 30, 2020.

State of Kansas, Chautauqua County, Subpoena, August 24, 1896. Kansas Historical Society. Kansas vs James Burgess and others. To Sheriff Payne in Oklahoma. Witnesses for the Defense, G.M. Atherton, Frank Atherton and Fred New. Retrieved June 30, 2020.

State of Kansas, Chautauqua County, Subpoena, August 28, 1896. Kansas Historical Society. Habeas Corpus for James Burgess, Theo Cox, William Leckliter and Mark McBee for State witnesses; John W. Oliver, Art Smith, S. Whitlock. Retrieved June 30, 2020.

State of Kansas, Chautauqua County, Application, August 28, 1896. Kansas Historical Society. Kansas vs James Burgess and others. To District Court of Chautauqua County. Defense request for deposition of, Asa Amos Greer in Moscow, Idaho. Retrieved June 30, 2020.

State of Kansas, Chautauqua County, Kansas Historical Society. Kansas vs James Burgess and others. List of witness names for the State. Retrieved June 30, 2020. No date.

State of Kansas, Chautauqua County, Kansas Historical Society. Kansas vs James Burgess, Theo Cox, William Leckliter, Mark McBee, F.S. Olney and John F. New. Counter Affidavit. Statement from residents of Jefferson Township in Chautauqua County that the defendants can have a fair trial in that county. Joe H. Powell first duly sworn for Hendricks, Chautauqua County. August 31, 1896.

(There are many such documents filed by the state to counter the change of venue).

State of Kansas, Chautauqua County, Kansas Historical Society. Kansas vs James Burgess and others .Petition for change of venue August 31, 1896 at 9:45 am by defendants. Retrieved June 30, 2020.

State of Kansas, Chautauqua County, Kansas Historical Society. Kansas vs James Burgess and others. Deposition of telegraph operator from Howard, John Kane September 1, 1896. Retrieved June 30, 2020.

State of Kansas, Chautauqua County, September 1, 1896. Kansas Historical Society. Kansas vs James Burgess and others. To District Court of Chautauqua County. Request for additional state witnesses unknown at time of filing. James Wallace, Same Berry, Samuel Hartzell and [Illegible-Joy?] McGrew Retrieved June 30, 2020.

State of Kansas, Chautauqua County, Kansas Historical Society. Kansas vs James Burgess, Theo Cox, William Leckliter, Mark McBee, F.S. Olney and John F. New. Journal Entry 998 for hearing September 1 to 5, 1896. List of jurors. James Reynolds, Everett E. Turner, Samuel G. Shirk, Iain N. Drake, Charles A. Dale, John Wilkinson, John Chittendon, James W. Uhls, David Franklin Arbaugh, James Tolson Botts, and J.W. Laverly.

State of Kansas, Chautauqua County, Subpoena, September 2, 1896. Kansas Historical Society. Habeas Corpus for James Burgess, Theo Cox, William Leckliter and Mark McBee for State witnesses; Mrs. J.W. McDaniel, William Price, F. McMartin, Aaron Glum, John W. Oliver, Joseph Butts, J.W. McDaniel. Retrieved June 30, 2020. (Not found, Riley Glander)

State of Kansas, Chautauqua County, Subpoena, September 2, 1896. Kansas Historical Society. Kansas vs James Burgess and others. Witnesses for the Defense, Grant Way, William Foreman and Philip Gephart. Retrieved June 30, 2020.

State of Kansas, Chautauqua County, Kansas Historical Society. Kansas vs James Burgess and others .Petition for change of venue September 2, 1896 defendants. Five pages. States case for inability to receive a fair trial based on articles in the Times Star and general attitude generated from those account by Chautauqua County residents. News articles attached to original petition and forty-two affidavits from residents proving prejudice. Retrieved June 30, 2020.

State of Kansas, Chautauqua County, Kansas Historical Society. Kansas vs James Burgess and others.

Motion to Endorse Names on Petition. September 2, 1896. County Attorney McBrian seeking to endorse Thomas Mitchell as a witness.

State of Kansas, Chautauqua County, Kansas Historical Society. Kansas vs F.S. Olney and others.

September 2, 1896. Petition for change of venue.

State of Kansas, Chautauqua County, Kansas Historical Society. Kansas vs F. S. Olney and others.

September 2, 1896. Affidavit for change of venue, Thomas Lawson and list of 41 others.

State of Kansas, Chautauqua County, Subpoena, September 3, 1896. Kansas Historical Society. Kansas vs James Burgess and others. Witness for the State, Robert Swain. Retrieved June 30, 2020.

State of Kansas, Chautauqua County, Kansas Historical Society. Kansas vs James Burgess and others.

Exhibit A, September 4, 1896. Retrieved June 30, 2020

State of Kansas, Chautauqua County, Kansas Historical Society. Kansas vs James Burgess and others.

Note excusing a Mrs. A.C. High from jury duty by Dr. S.H. Murphy of Thayer, Kansas. No date.

State of Kansas, Chautauqua County, Kansas Historical Society. Kansas vs James Burgess, Theo Cox, William Leckliter, Mark McBee, F.S. Olney and John F. New. Counter Affidavit. Statement from residents of Jefferson Township in Chautauqua County that the defendants can have a fair trial in that county. By township trustee, Austin Brown. No date.

State of Kansas, Chautauqua County, Kansas Historical Society. Kansas vs James Burgess, Theo Cox, William Leckliter, Mark McBee, F.S. Olney and John F. New. Recognizance for Theo Cox. Bond of six thousand dollars to appear for trial at Greenwood County for Frazer murder. September 6, 1896.

State of Kansas, Chautauqua County, Kansas Historical Society. Kansas vs James Burgess, Theo Cox, William Leckliter, Mark McBee, F.S. Olney and John F. New. Recognizance for Theo Cox. Bond of six thousand dollars to appear for trial at Greenwood County for Frazer murder. September 6, 1896.

State of Kansas, Chautauqua County, Kansas Historical Society. Kansas vs James Burgess, Theo Cox, William Leckliter, Mark McBee, F.S. Olney and John F. New. Counter Affidavit by R.H. Nichols regarding change of venue. Refers to numbers of citizens being in attendance to the 1894 hearing and acknowledge of case. Focus on activities of H.G. Mosier and Pinkerton detective. September 7, 1896.

State of Kansas, Chautauqua County, Kansas Historical Society. Kansas vs James Burgess, Theo Cox, William Leckliter, Mark McBee, F.S. Olney and John F. New. Recognizance for Mark McBee. Bond of six thousand dollars to appear for trial at Greenwood County for Frazer murder. September 8, 1896.

State of Kansas, Chautauqua County, Kansas Historical Society. Kansas vs James Burgess, Theo Cox, William Leckliter, Mark McBee, F.S. Olney and John F. New. Recognizance for William Leckliter. Bond of six thousand dollars to appear for trial at Greenwood County for Frazer murder paid by John E. Brogan of Elk County. September 8, 1896. List of witnesses and monetary amounts; J.B. Dolan $1000, J.W. Hamon $250.00, S.B. Johnson $290.00, J.A. Stillman $250.00, S.D. Lewis $500.00, W.M. (illegible), H.P. McBee $1000.00, E.A. Piercy $250.00, Dan Doughtery $500.00, J.W. Bacus $500.00, John Edward Barnaby $500.00, John Bounham $250.00, C.T. Braughman $150.00, J.K (illegible) $500.00.

State of Kansas, Chautauqua County, Kansas Historical Society. Kansas vs James Burgess, Theo Cox, William Leckliter, Mark McBee, F.S. Olney and John F. New. Recognizance for Theo Cox. Bond of one thousand dollars to appear for trial at Greenwood County for Frazer murder paid by John E. Brogan of Elk County. September 9, 1896.

List of witnesses and monetary amounts; W.M. Lenwood $500.00, H.P. McBee $1000.00, J.J. Hamilton $1000, Albert (illegible) $500.00, J.M. Beckworth $2000.00, T.M. Carter $500.00, Samuel Donelson, $100.00. No date.

State of Kansas, Chautauqua County, Kansas Historical Society. Kansas vs James Burgess, Theo Cox, William Leckliter, Mark McBee, F.S. Olney and John F. New. Recognizance for James Burgess. Bond of six thousand dollars to appear for trial at Greenwood County for Frazer murder paid by John E. Brogan of Elk County. September 9, 1896. List of witnesses and monetary amounts; S.J. Johnson $2000, Milo D. Stevens, $1000, Patrick Looby $1500, Ed Dryer $1000, Samuel Wilson $1000, D.B. Worley $500, Charles Kennedy $1000, Daniel W. Hanes $500, N.J. Williams $2000, G.W. Sharpe $1000.

State of Kansas, Chautauqua County, Kansas Historical Society. Kansas vs James Burgess, Theo Cox, William Leckliter, Mark McBee, F.S. Olney and John F. New. Recognizance for F.S. Olney. Bond of five thousand dollars to appear for trial at Greenwood County for Frazer murder. Paid by J.N. Carr. September 10, 1896.

State of Kansas, Chautauqua County, Jury Instructions for Frazer murder trial 1896 Kansas vs James Burgess and others. Kansas Historical Society. First degree murder charges for Burgess Jury in Chautauqua County by Judge Jackson. No date.

State of Kansas, Chautauqua County, Motion to Dismiss No. 338 Kansas vs James Burgess and others. Kansas Historical Society. County Attorney McBrian. After two trials State moves to dismiss at that time. No date given.

State of Kansas, Chautauqua County, Motion for Separate Trial. Kansas vs James Burgess and others. Kansas Historical Society. Burgess requests separate hearing and trial. R.H. Nichols and T.N. King for defendants. No date.

Books by D.A. Chadwick

Also by D.A. Chadwick

Retribution
God Barks
Rennes le Chateau: The Road to Sion
The Good Nazi
The Grass Widow
The Chimera Project
Paper Memories: Distant Voices of the Third Reich Volumes 1 and 2
The Singing Nun: The Life and Death of Soeur Sourire
The 1st Field Hospital: The Experiences of T-4 Robert U. Shepard in the Southwest Pacific

D.A. Chadwick is the author of eleven fiction and nonfiction books and a professional translator of French, German and Dutch to English.. She resides in the Midwestern United States.

D.A. Chadwick

www.ingramcontent.com/pod-product-compliance
Lightning Source LLC
Chambersburg PA
CBHW071358290426
44108CB00014B/1600